Handmade
Underground
JEWELRY

First published in USA and Canada by
Wiley Publishing, Inc., Hoboken, New Jersey

Copyright © 2009 Elwin Street Limited
Conceived and produced by
Elwin Street Limited
144 Liverpool Road
London N1 1LA
www.elwinstreet.com

For general information on our other products and services or to obtain technical support please contact our Customer Care Department within the U.S. at (877) 762-2974, outside the U.S. at (317) 572-3993 or fax (317) 572-4002.

Wiley also publishes its books in a variety of electronic formats. Some content that appears in print may not be available in electronic books. For more information about Wiley products, please visit our web site at www.wiley.com.

ISBN: 978-0-470-50436-9

Printed in China

10 —9 —8 —7 —6 —5 —4 —3 —2 —1

Handmade Underground JEWELRY

25 Fun Projects for All Occasions

Shannon LeVart

WILEY
wiley.com

CONTENTS

INTRODUCTION

Flip through the pages of any fashion magazine and you will see an impressive display of finely crafted designer jewelry. Choose a piece that takes your fancy, look past the high price, and you see a name. This is the name of the person who conceived that design and gave it life. Driven by a passion to create, every jewelry designer starts with the simple act of making something with his or her hands, and this is something you can do, too—express yourself by using your own hands to create a hip jewelry style of your own.

As a student and young adult, I spent my time between classes and jobs on the floor of libraries and bookstores, pouring over pictures, marveling at the way a small pile of beads and findings could turn into beautiful jewelry. In 1989, handmade was the way to go because I didn't have the money to purchase what I felt expressed my own unique style. I have been designing and making my own jewelry ever since, and the experience has been life changing. In these times of mass production and assembly-line manufacturing it's all too easy to go out and spend your money on cheaply made goods, but I am able to create something from scratch. This is a great source of personal pride for me: Handmade is a part of my identity, my creativity, and has grown into something tangible for the world to see and relate to.

You can get into this "do-it-yourself" mindset about your own jewelry. Using just a small number of basic techniques, you will find new and wonderful ways to identify your own personal style and express yourself. And you'll find it cheaper and more fun than buying ready-mades: Pick out striking vintage elements to mix with modern metals; spend time searching for eclectic focal points that set you apart from the crowd; play around with beads to find unique colorways and combinations.

Shannon LeVart

MATERIALS, TOOLS, TECHNIQUES

The 25 projects in this book cover a range of jewelry-making techniques and styles—from beading, knotting, and wire wrapping to sewing and mixed media. Each project is easy to follow, with in-process steps and illustrations, so that you can view the work in stages. You can make the pieces as they are—or use them as a springboard from which to explore and experiment in making pieces to your own designs. Variations on projects are dotted throughout the book to inspire you to adapt and personalize your creations.

Over the following pages you'll find summaries of the materials used in the projects, descriptions of all the tools you need and the jobs they do, as well as foolproof instructions for measuring up. You will discover techniques that are commonly used throughout the book, and step-by-step instructions for how to perfect these. This will give you a great base from which to begin creating unique, handmade jewelry.

BEADS, CHAINS, AND RIBBONS

The variety of beads available for jewelry making is endless. Combine this with the different chains and charms that you can now buy, and there is no limit to what you can make. Here is a summary of the materials used for the projects in this book, which provides a solid base from which to explore and experiment in making pieces to your own designs. Many of the materials in this book are given in metric measurements, which is how they are typically sold.

Bead Types

Seed beads: Predominantly used for bead weaving, these can also feature in simpler, more modern designs, and range in size from 1mm to 4mm. They are sold by measurement, according to

Seed beads

how many beads make 1 in. (2.5cm) when strung together. For example 6/0 (pronounced "six aught") means that six beads make 1 in. (2.5cm), each measuring approximately 4mm. Seed beads are available in many colors, from opaque to transparent. Some are lined with a different color, others with a metallic finish. An exterior coating of a metallic film adds a luster to seed beads called aurora borealis (a/b). There are several types of seed bead: Bugle beads

Seed beads

are longer and have sharp-cut ends; charlotte-cut beads are faceted; hex-cut beads have a hexagon-shaped cylinder.

Glass beads: There are many glass beads available, several of which have been used in the projects in this book. Available in every color,

Briolette glass beads

Red glass beads

Semi-precious stone beads

Pearls

shape, and size known to man, glass beads can add sparkle, texture, and, in the case of artisan beads, value. Faceted glass beads have multiple cuts on the surface; Czech glass beads—made in the Czech Republic—are known for their variety of shapes and quality; iridescent glass beads have a fire-polished coating, which gives them a multihued surface.

Semi-precious stone beads: There are many natural stones, found in a host of different colors. Some of them are "precious" (diamonds and rubies); some are "semi-precious" (quartz, chalcedony, jade, moonstone, labradorite). A cabochon is a stone that has been cut, ground flat on the bottom, and domed or faceted on top.

Pearls: It is important when purchasing pearls to pay attention to what you are buying: Glass pearls are lovely and offer a nice alternative to the more costly freshwater pearls, but their beauty does fade once the pearl coating begins to rub off.

Freshwater pearls cost a few dollars more but their luster takes decades to fade. Mother-of-pearl is taken from within the shell, cut, and shaped. Some are dyed beautiful colors, while natural mother-of-pearl is light brown, swirled with white.

Crystal beads: These are lead crystal glass beads with precise machine-cut facets, which sparkle like no other beads.

Crystal beads

Acrylic, Lucite, and resin beads: Inexpensive and lightweight, acrylic beads have been used in beaded jewelry for decades. Lucite was very popular in the 1930s, as an alternative

Acrylic, Lucite, and resin beads

to the more expensive Bakelite. One of the most popular types of Lucite is the moonglow, a shimmering bead that has a middle band of a lighter color than the rest of the bead.

Moonglow

Cloisonné: This term describes beads that have been decorated with metal and enamel. Filigree metal is used to outline flowers or patterns on the surface of a bead, which are then colored-in with enamel glazes.

Metals

Vermeil: This is a product that is made with a base of sterling silver and is coated or plated on its surface with gold.

Brass filigrees: Are flat brass shapes with an ornamental openwork design.

Vermeil

Hill Tribe beads: Are fine silver beads handcrafted by the Karen Hill Tribe of Northern Thailand. Intricate in detail and crafted using methods passed down from generations, they add a tremendous amount of value and style to handmade jewelry.

Hill Tribe beads

Bali silver: These are lovely handcrafted sterling-silver beads with tiny wire detailing created by artisans in Bali in the traditional Balinese style.

Chain

Figaro chain: A style of chain that has a pattern of two or three small circular links with one elongated oval link.

Curb-link chain: A type of chain in which the links are oval and twisted so that they lie flat.

Ribbons and Fabric

Grosgrain ribbon: A type of ribbon with a thick, slightly stiff ribbed feel.

Felt: A soft, matted fabric, usually made from wool.

FINDINGS

Findings are all those pretty little bits and pieces that pull your jewelry together—clasps, ear posts, ring bases, and pin backs.

Clasps: Used for securing a necklace or brooch for wearing, there are many different clasp styles available, and it is easy to get overwhelmed. You need to consider the size of beads you are stringing before choosing your clasp—the larger the beads, the more balanced your design will look with a larger size clasp. A lobster-claw clasp hooks into a jump ring and is the most secure; a toggle clasp is a pretty, decorative way to end a design and most people can clasp them by themselves; pearl or filigree clasps have the added security of an inner hook. There are hook and "S" clasps available in a variety of finishes and embellishments, in addition to multiple-strand clasps used for finishing off designs created from more than one strand of beads.

Lobster-claw clasp

Extender chain

Extender chains: Small lengths of chain attached to a clasp to give the wearer the option of lengthening the necklace.

Jump rings: Closed circles of hard wire used for attaching clasps to a strand of beads. A range of sizes is useful for a range of different clasps.

Jump ring

Crimp beads

Bead tip

Ear wires

Pin backs

Crimp beads: Hollow cylinder beads used for attaching beading wire securely to a clasp (done using crimping pliers). Available in two sizes—4mm and 2mm—the smaller beads are used for all projects requiring crimping in this book.

Bead tips (also known as *knot covers*): Little clam-like components used for closing over a knot on the knotting cord when attaching the cord to jump rings on a clasp.

Ear wires: Preformed components that slide into pierced ears. Available in all shapes and sizes, in both base and precious metals. Common types include kidney wires, which hook behind the ear; lever-back wires, which operate with a spring closure; French wires, which use rubber stoppers at the back for securing; and ear hoops.

Ear posts: A style of earring with a small prong and backing. There are decorative posts available with flowers, hearts, and other designs. Some include a loop at the bottom from which to hang beads and charms, others have a flat surface on which to glue flat-backed items.

Head pins: Either with a ball end, flat end, or flower end, these wire pieces are used for creating drops for earrings or charms. The gauge of the wire needs careful consideration with the size of the bead being used.

Pin backs: Flat surfaces with a pin mechanism, on which to attach jewelry .

TOOLS AND SUPPLIES

Jewelry making is one of those crafts that can be made easier with a few handy tools and supplies. Here are a few things that you will find yourself using on a regular basis.

Work Surfaces

Bead boards: Flat boards with channels or grooves—usually with measurements—for laying beads in while designing a piece of jewelry.

Thick cloth: A scrap of faux suede or felt laid out next to your bead area to help keep extra beads from rolling away as you work on a design.

Wire-wrapping jig: A flat surface with drilled holes in a grid pattern and pegs of different sizes that fit into the holes. Wire-wrapping jigs are used for bending wire into different shapes around the pegs, to create ear wires for earrings, for example.

Hand Tools

Chain-nose pliers: Smooth, pointed pliers used for gripping, and useful for all forms of jewelry making. You will need two pairs for some tasks.

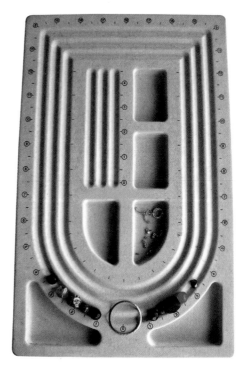

Bead board

Wire cutters: Smaller, pointed cutters used for cutting beading wire. Larger, less pointed cutters are needed for cutting metal wire for wire wrapping.

Crimping pliers: Special pliers with grooves inside the tip. The first, a double groove, is used for pressing a seam into a crimp bead; the second groove is used for closing the seam.

Half-round-nose pliers: Semi-circular pliers used for forming wire rings or hoops. These are also useful for reshaping jump rings that have lost their circle.

Flush cutters: Special cutters that can handle cutting heavy-gauge and half-hard wire perfectly flat.

Awl: A narrow, sharp-ended tool used when knotting cord. It helps to tighten a knot by guiding the cording into place.

Scissors: Small, pointed-tip scissors for cutting cord and thread.

Jeweler's file: A small, thin, fine file used to remove burrs (sharp metal pieces) from the ends of cut wire. An emery board can be used on the thinner gauge wires, such as 20 or 24 gauge.

Hand needles or *sharps*: Available in sizes ranging from 1–10, sharps in any size can be used.

Beading needle: A special needle that is thin enough to fit into the inner holes of tiny beads. Usually a longer than normal sewing needle to make gathering several beads at once easier.

Awl

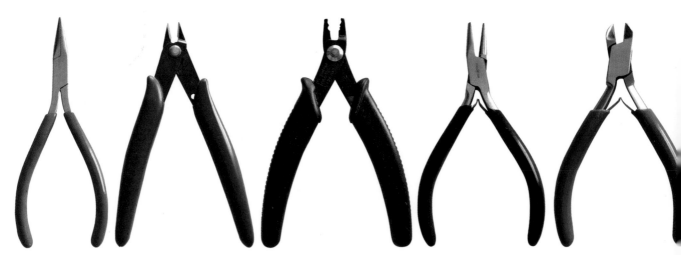

Chain-nose pliers   Wire cutters   Crimping pliers   Half-round-nose pliers   Flush cutters

Measuring Tools

Ring sizers: Plastic rings embossed with different ring sizes.

Ring mandrel: Marked with whole and half ring sizes, this tool is invaluable when it comes to making wire-wrapped rings, and can be used to start the process off, but also for double-checking progress, as you work.

Adhesives

Epoxy: A very powerful adhesive. Projects using this glue will need to be left overnight to set.

Fabric glue: A quick-drying and safe glue used for holding fabrics together.

Jeweler's cement: A strong, clear-drying adhesive used for gluing the knots inside bead tips. This sets within a few seconds. Clear nail polish can work just as well.

Ring mandrel

Stringing Materials

Sewing thread: Used for sewing on light- and medium-weight cotton, rayon, and linen. Cotton thread in a medium thickness (size 50) is available in a wide range of colors.

Prepared nylon or silk cord: Used for knotting beads, cord comes in a wide variety of colors to both match and contrast with the beads you have chosen to knot. Cord that comes prepared with a stiff, twisted needle is the most convenient option for knotting beads. Most freshwater pearls use size Nos. 0 through 3; most other beads will slide easily on Nos. 5 and 6.

Approximate sizes of each cord for the number on the packaging:

No. 0: 0.30mm (.012 in.)	No. 6: 0.70mm (.028 in.)
No. 1: 0.35mm (.014 in.)	No. 7: 0.75mm (.030 in.)
No. 2: 0.45mm (.018 in.)	No. 8: 0.80mm (.032 in.)
No. 3: 0.50mm (.020 in.)	No. 10: 0.90mm (.036 in.)
No. 4: 0.60mm (.024 in.)	No. 12: 0.98mm (.039 in.)
No. 5: 0.65mm (.026 in.)	No. 14: 1.02mm (.040 in.)

Beading wire (also known as *cable* or *tiger tail*): A durable, nylon-coated, stainless-steel wire, available in several thicknesses. The higher the number listed on the spool, the thicker the wire. All of the beading projects in this book have been made with .018 in. flexible beading wire.

Stainless-steel, brass, sterling-silver, and gold-filled wire: Wire is available in three degrees of hardness: dead soft, half hard, and full hard. Dead soft is useful for wire-wrapped beaded necklaces and earrings. However, it is easily bent and will not keep its shape. Half-hard wire is a dead-soft wire that has been partially worked so that it has gained some hardness and durability. Although a little bit more difficult to wrap, it is ideal for wire-wrapped rings and bracelets, and jewelry pieces that take on more wear and tear. Full-hard wire is best left to metal smiths, who hammer and shape it into bangles, neck cuffs, and soldered rings.

The thicker the wire, the lower the number. As a rough guide, 28 gauge is good for wire-wrapping freshwater pearls or precious stones like chalcedony, because it is thin enough to fit in the tiny holes drilled in these softer, more expensive stones; 20-gauge wire is thicker and stiffer and better suited to creating ear wires and rings, as it will keep its shape.

American Wire Gauges

Wire Gauge	Inches	Millimeters
14	0.064	1.63
15	0.057	1.45
16	0.051	1.30
17	0.045	1.14
18	0.040	1.02
19	0.036	0.914
20	0.032	0.813
21	0.029	0.737
22	0.025	0.635
24	0.020	0.508
25	0.018	0.455
26	0.016	0.406
28	0.013	0.320
30	0.010	0.254

British Wire Gauges

Wire Gauge	British Imperial Standard (S.W.G.)	Birmingham or Stubs
14	.080 in.	.083 in.
15	.072 in.	.072 in.
16	.064 in.	.065 in.
17	.056 in.	.058 in.
18	.048 in.	.049 in.
19	.040 in.	.042 in.
20	.036 in.	.035 in.
21	.032 in.	.032 in.
22	.028 in.	.028 in.
23	.024 in.	.025 in.
24	.022 in.	.022 in.
25	.020 in.	.020 in.
26	.018 in.	.018 in.
27	.0164 in.	.016 in.
28	.0148 in.	.014 in.
29	.0136 in.	.013 in.
30	.0124 in.	.012 in.

MEASURING UP

It is up to you to decide how long to make a piece of jewelry—say you want a vintage locket at bust level or an anklet that goes around your leg twice. It is frustrating to get it wrong, or to have to start again, so always measure carefully before beginning any new jewelry project.

1 Hold up a flexible measuring tape to your neckline, wrist, ankle, or finger, to determine where you want the jewelry to lie. Note that measurement.

2 Working from the clasp backward, design your piece, using a bead board to assemble the jewelry components. (Example: If your clasp measures ¾ in. (2cm), you will need to cut a length of chain at 15¼ in. (38cm) to create a 16 in. (40cm) necklace.)

3 Check your jewelry measurements frequently by holding pieces up to your neckline, wrist, ankle, or finger as you work.

4 Make necessary adjustments before finishing off a piece.

Bear in mind that jump rings, crimps, wire wrapping, and knot covers all add to the overall measurement of a completed piece. Keep track of the size of the findings and remember to include the added measurement when laying out your final design.

For example: Your clasp measures 1 in. (2.5cm). In order to attach it to a strand of beads, you need two jump rings and two crimp beads, both of which will add ⅛ in. (2–3mm), to your finished length. You also need to allow for the wire loop that you make in attaching the jump ring to the clasp. These are minute measurements, but they add up and can make the difference between a piece that is well loved and worn often, or pushed to the back of a jewelry box and never worn at all.

JEWELRY-MAKING TECHNIQUES

The projects in this book use three very basic jewelry-making techniques: beading, knotting, and wire wrapping. Within those techniques are a number of steps that get used time and again. The most frequent are described below for easy reference.

Crimping

Crimping is the method used for securing beads strung on beading wire (see page 18). The idea is to thread the wire through a crimp bead at each end of a piece of jewelry, before attaching it to a clasp, and to press the crimp bead flat using crimping pliers, so trapping the wires inside.

What you need

- Crimp beads
- Clasp
- Chain-nose pliers
- Crimping pliers
- Wire cutters

Once happy with a piece of strung jewelry, you can add the clasp to complete the design. You should have a loose overhand knot at each end of the beading wire. Starting at one end, untie the knot and slide on a crimp bead (see Fig. 1).

Loop the end of the wire through a jump ring on one side of the clasp, and thread the beading wire back through the crimp bead (see Fig. 2). Pull on the extra wire using a pair of chain-nose pliers to shorten the loop that connects the beading wire to the clasp.

Fig. 1   Fig. 2

Get it right!

If you wear your beaded jewelry frequently, re-string pieces every six months to prevent an unexpected break and the scattering of beautiful beads!

Position the crimp bead inside the second notch in the crimping pliers (the one closest to you as you hold the tool in your hand), and close the crimping pliers around the crimp bead. As you do this, the groove in the crimping tool separates the two wires in the crimp bead (see Fig. 3).

Fig. 3

Now position the same crimp bead in the first notch of the crimping pliers, facing the same way as before. Close the crimping pliers again,

Fig. 4

flattening the crimp bead in an even, creased tube, with both wires securely pressed inside (see Fig. 4).

Attach the opposite end of the beading wire to the second jump ring on the clasp in exactly the same way. Pull the extra wire tightly using the chain-nose pliers so there is very little slack between the beads (see Fig. 5). Use the wire cutters to trim away the excess wire as close to the crimp bead as you can.

Fig. 5

Opening and Closing Jump Rings

A good number of projects in this book use jump rings—small hoops attached to clasps and onto which you need to thread a strung or knotted piece of jewelry. Whatever the construction of a piece of jewelry, jump rings invariably need to be opened and closed during the finishing stages. Here's how to do it.

What you need

• Chain-nose pliers (2 pairs)

To open a jump ring, grip the ring between two pairs of chain-nose pliers and push each pair of pliers gently in opposite directions (see Fig. 6). Do not pull the ring apart, as this will weaken the metal, distorting the circle shape.

Fig. 6

Close the jump ring the same way you opened it, pushing the pliers in the opposite direction now, until the two ends of the ring meet and form a seam.

Knotting

Knotting is a technique used for stringing beads on cord. The technique is really simple: You simply string each bead in turn, tying an overhand knot after each one. Using an awl to help you, it is then easy to push the knot flush against the bead, pulling it tight at the same time. (See chapter 3 for projects that use knotting)

What you need

• Bead tips
• Prepared silk or nylon cording with twisted needle included
• Awl
• Beads
• Jeweler's cement
• Chain-nose pliers
• Scissors

Each knotting project starts and ends with a bead tip, which then hooks into the jump ring of the clasp. Your first knot should therefore be a double knot, at one end of the cord, over which you slide the bead tip, facing outward, so that you can close it over the knot at the end of the project (see Fig. 7).

Fig. 7

Tie an overhand knot close to the bead tip, and insert the awl into the loose knot (see Fig. 8).

Fig. 8

Use the awl to push the knot down toward the bead tip while holding onto the untied end of the cord with your other hand. The idea is to slide the knot up flush against the bead tip (see Fig. 9).

Fig. 9

Keeping the knot up against the bead tip, slide the end of your awl out of the knot and immediately push the knot against the bead tip using your fingers. Now you can string your beads, knotting in

Fig. 10

exactly the same way after each one (see Fig. 10).

Slide another bead tip onto the cord after your last knotted bead and tie a double knot, using your awl to ensure a tight fit. Coat the double knots inside the bead tips with jeweler's cement (see Fig. 11) and press the bead tip closed using chain-nose pliers. Cut away the excess cording with sharp scissors.

Fig. 11

Get it right!

If your knots have gaps between, you can use the sharp end of the awl to pick the knots apart and retie them.

Wire Wrapping

This is a must-have technique for securely connecting beads, findings, and other elements into your jewelry designs, and involves making wire links for the various components to hook onto. The technique may seem challenging at first but all it takes is a little practice. You won't believe how fast you get used to using the pliers—like a second pair of hands—and you will soon be incorporating this technique into just about every design you create! (See chapters 4 and 5 for projects that use this technique.)

What you need

- Stainless-steel, brass, sterling-silver, or gold-filled wire, dead soft (see "Tools and Supplies" on page 15)
- Flush cutters
- Beads and other jewelry components
- Half-round-nose pliers
- Chain-nose pliers

Use flush cutters to cut four times the bead length you are wrapping from your choice of wire. Thread one end of the wire through the bead, and hold this secure in one hand as you work the opposite end of the wire.

Use the half-round-nose pliers to make a bend in the wire, at a right angle, close to the bead. You want to create an upside down "L" shape (see Fig. 12).

Fig. 12

Use your fingers, or a pair of chain-nose pliers, to pull the wire around the half-round-nose pliers, creating a small loop (see Fig. 13).

Fig. 13

Get it right!

It is worth practicing this technique using brass or steel wire before using the more expensive gold-filled or sterling-silver alternatives.

Fig. 14

Keeping the half-round-nose pliers inside the loop you have just made, use your fingers or the chain-nose pliers to grasp the extra wire and wind it two to three times around the base of the loop you have just made, to form a tidy spiral. Cut away the excess wire using the flush cutters and press the cut end into the wire wrap using the chain-nose pliers. Carry out the same process at both ends of the wire passing through your bead (see Fig. 14).

Sewing

Often overlooked these days in favor of more modern materials, sewing can add a lovely texture to jewelry projects. There is also the added benefit of using a strong thread, knotted and coated in glue, which can last a lifetime.

What you need

- Sewing thread
- Sewing needle

Basic stitch: Cut a length of thread that closely matches the fabric you are sewing. Thread the needle and double-knot the ends together. Start at a place in your project that can be hidden by a bead, clasp, or other design element. Always start by coming up from the back of the fabric and going down through the front.

For running stitch and basting, simply make small stitches in a line.

BEADING

CHAPTER 2

ere are five high-impact projects that are low on the difficulty scale. Using simple wire is one of the most durable ways to string beads and it's so easy, you'll find yourself reaching for it again and again.

Give yourself approximately 30 minutes to complete each of the first four projects. The fifth project, although more time consuming, is no more difficult to make; its completion will take closer to three hours. These time estimations include organizing your tools and supplies, laying out your beads, and stringing and finishing the piece. You could be wearing your new jewelry tonight!

The Jewelry

The single-strand Color Band Rings are a great way to practice and get a feel for crimping without wasting a lot of wire or crimp beads. Once you are forming an even tube when crimping, you will feel more confident about taking on the longer Crimson Flash Necklace. The Siren's City Bracelet is simply a strand of beading wire cut in half, and then strung and crimped to accommodate a hammered brass circle element—the focus of the piece. Use the Ruby Pheasant Earrings as shoulder dusters for a glamorous effect, taking note that anything that can hold up to daily wear and has a stem can be crimped alongside beading wire. The Tiered Festival Necklace is perfect for shimmering against a little black dress or adding a sparkle by peeking out of a business blouse. This project will show you how to layer your strands and make the most out of a clasp. The projects use red, gold, and black for drama, but you can recreate these pieces in your own favorite colors, adapting them to a variety of functions, day or night.

COLOR BAND RINGS

Expect to grow addicted to these easy, colorful bands of beads. Comfortable to wear and available in every color under the sun, you will soon have stacks and stacks to wear with every outfit. Made from small seed beads in multiple sizes, you can wear these fun rings singly or in stacks all the way up your finger. Assign meanings to each of your favorite colors and give them to your closest friends, or make them in solid gold or silver for a funkier look. Get ready for a lot of people to want them! This project makes five rings.

Skill level ★ Approximate completion time: **30 minutes**

What you need

- 5 in. (12.5cm) pieces of 0.18 beading wire (x5)
- 2mm gold-filled crimp beads (x5)
- Red 10/0 or smaller seed beads (approx. 50)
- Gold 12/0 faceted seed beads (approx. 150)
- Black 10/0 or smaller seed beads (approx. 50)
- Flexible measuring tape
- Wire cutters
- Bead board
- Crimping pliers

Get it right!

Make sure your rings fit properly by measuring your finger slightly bent, and always remember to double-check the fit before crimping and finishing your color bands.

Measuring

Measure your finger using the flexible measuring tape (see "Measuring Up" on page 19) and use wire cutters to cut double the length of wire that you need for a completed piece.

Tie one end in a loose overhand knot, but do not tighten. This is a temporary knot that you will cut away later, and simply keeps the beads from falling off while you are stringing your design.

Slide on a crimp bead.

Stringing

Lay out the seed beads in the channels of the bead board to the length of your finger measurement, in an arrangement you like, and allowing 2mm for the crimp bead.

Begin stringing the beads until you have reached the measurement you need.

Thread the unknotted end of the beading wire into the crimp bead (heading in the opposite direction this time) and pull the wire so that the beads form a tight circle (see Fig. 1).

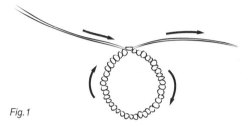

Fig. 1

Slide the uncrimped ring onto your finger to double-check the size.

Add or remove beads until you have a comfortable fit.

Crimping

Once you have the correct size you can begin the crimping process (see "Crimping" on page 20).

Place the crimp bead into the second notch inside the tip of the crimping pliers.

Squeeze gently, until the crimp has formed a seam in the crimp, separating the two wires.

Now turn the crimp bead so that the seam faces outward and place it in the first notch of the crimping pliers.

Press until the crimp has completely closed.

Finishing

Bend any surplus wire up and away from the seed beads and trim using the wire cutters.

Variation

This ring style can be enhanced by adding a special focal bead at the center of the seed beads. The variation here shows a ring created using 2mm sterling-silver beads and a fabulous Swarovski crystal in the color Vitrail.

CRIMSON FLASH NECKLACE

Crimson-colored glass nuggets are the perfect choice for combining with the ornate, filigree stamping of this large brass medallion. The faceted, smooth-polished beads flash brilliantly when they catch the light. They are readily available online and come in a variety of colors, including emerald green, aquamarine blue, and even rose-alabaster pink! The two small, matte-black seed beads flanking the jump ring of the brass medallion prevent it from scraping the red glass and allow it to lay flat on your body when wearing the piece.

Skill level ★ Approximate completion time: **30 minutes**

What you need

- 15 in. (38cm) strand temporarily strung 22mm red glass nuggets
- Black 8/0 seed beads (x2)
- 2½ in. (6.35cm) brass filigree stamping
- 22 in. (56cm) piece of 0.18 beading wire
- 6mm gold-filled jump ring
- 2mm gold-filled crimp beads (x2)

- 28 x 10mm vermeil hook clasp with jump rings attached
- Flexible measuring tape
- Wire cutters
- Bead board
- Chain-nose pliers (2 pairs)
- Crimping pliers

Measuring

Measure for your completed piece using the flexible measuring tape (see "Measuring Up" on page 19) and lay out your faceted red glass beads to the correct measurement on the bead board.

Add ¼ in. (6mm) at the center of the red beads to make room for your black seed beads and brass medallion.

Decide on the length of necklace you want to make and add 6 in. (16cm) allowance for ease of making. Cut the wire using wire cutters and tie a loose overhand knot near one end of the beading wire. The necklace shown measures 16 in. (40cm), but you can easily adjust the length by adding small seed beads at the back of the necklace—right before the clasp—or spaced between each glass nugget.

Stringing

String your beads to half the measurement, in this case 8 in. (20cm), and slide on one black seed bead, knot the opposite end of the beading wire so the beads stay on and set your strand down.

Use two pairs of chain-nose pliers to open a jump ring (see "Opening and Closing Jump Rings" on page 22).

Thread the jump ring through the medallion at an open area in the filigree and close the jump ring the same way you opened it.

Untie the second knot in the beading wire, and string on the pendant (see Fig. 1).

Fig. 1

Now string the second black seed bead and then the remaining faceted red glass beads onto the wire.

Retie the open end of the beading wire.

Double-check the opposite end of your strung beads to make sure it is still securely tied. Now hold the necklace up to yourself to confirm it is the measurement you desire.

Make any adjustments necessary at this point by adding or removing beads. Always take the time to securely knot both ends of your necklace as you do this.

Crimping

Once you have determined that the measurement is correct, untie the knot at one end of the beading wire and slide on a crimp bead.

Now loop the wire through the jump ring on the male side of the vermeil hook clasp and then back through the crimp bead.

Tighten the wire, using chain-nose pliers, and crimp the crimp bead with the crimping pliers (see "Crimping" on page 20).

Trim off the extra beading wire.

Repeat the crimping process at the opposite end of your necklace, sliding a crimp bead onto the wire and threading the wire through the jump ring that the hook clasp latches into, and then back through the crimp bead.

Once you have crimped the bead, trim off the extra wire using wire cutters (see Fig. 2).

Fig. 2

SIREN'S CITY BRACELET

This design gives an instant impression of sophistication with its mix of steel gray, jet black, brilliant gold, and lipstick red—all a gorgeous backdrop for the geometric, hammered-brass focal point. Mixed bead bracelets are a wonderful way to use up extra beads you will inevitably find yourself collecting from various projects. This design uses tiny, faceted vermeil beads throughout the design to pull it all together, and the ring design of the hammered brass is echoed in the circle toggle clasp. Even though the finished piece uses so many different-shaped beads, the design flows cohesively.

Skill level ★ ★ Approximate completion time: **30 minutes**

What you need

- 6 in. (15cm) lengths of 0.18 beading wire (x2)
- 33mm hammered-brass ring finding
- 12mm vermeil toggle clasp with jump rings attached
- 2mm gold-filled crimp beads (x4)
- Clear, red, or black 8/0 seed beads (x12)
- 3mm faceted vermeil beads (x12)
- 12mm faceted black Czech-glass bead
- 12mm red crackle acrylic bead
- 17mm matte-black glass nugget bead

- 8mm faceted Czech fire-polished glass bead
- 10mm matte-black glass bead
- 8mm red-jade carved bead
- 15mm zebra-striped glass nugget bead
- 8mm matte-red ribbed-glass melon bead
- Flexible measuring tape
- Bead board
- Wire cutters
- Chain-nose pliers
- Crimping pliers

Measuring

First, decide where on your wrist you would like the bracelet to rest. Now measure your wrist using the flexible measuring tape (see "Measuring Up" on page 19). This style of bracelet looks best lying flat against the wrist.

The beaded section of the bracelet is made from two equal-length pieces of wire. To calculate these, subtract the diameter of the brass circle and the length of the toggle clasp from your chosen wrist length, and divide this figure by two.

The bracelet shown measures 7½ in. (19cm).

Lay out your beads on the bead board, arranging and rearranging until you have two groupings to fit the lengths you calculated in the previous step.

Assembling

Begin by stringing one crimp bead and six clear seed beads onto one length of beading wire.

Loop the wire through your brass focal point and back into the crimp bead.

Use the chain-nose pliers to pull on the short piece of beading wire until the crimp is tight up against the seed bead loop, and you have three seed beads either side of the brass focal point (see Fig. 1).

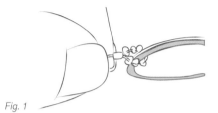

Fig. 1

Crimp the crimp bead (see "Crimping" on page 20) and repeat the process for the second length of beading wire.

Use the wire cutters to trim the short end of each length of beading wire.

You should now have two longer pieces of wire remaining on which to string the rest of your design, keeping the brass focal point centered in the middle (see Fig. 2).

Fig. 2

String the first length of beading wire as follows: One faceted vermeil, the faceted black glass, one vermeil, the red crackle acrylic, one vermeil, the matte-black glass nugget, one vermeil, the Czech fire-polished glass bead, one vermeil, and one crimp bead.

Knot this strand of beads loosely with an overhand knot.

String the second length of beading wire as follows: One vermeil, the matte-black glass bead, one vermeil, the carved red jade, one vermeil, the zebra-striped nugget bead, one vermeil, the matte-red ribbed-glass melon bead, one vermeil, and a crimp bead.

Knot this strand of beads loosely with an overhand knot.

Crimping

Begin the crimping process for both sides of the bracelet, looping the beading wire through the jump rings on the toggle clasp and back through the crimp bead.

Do not crimp the beads yet, but pull the wires tight using the chain-nose pliers and try on your bracelet to see if it fits comfortably. This example needed one more faceted vermeil bead to add a little bit more length.

Adjust your beads as necessary by adding or removing beads until you have a comfortable fit.

Finish the crimping process once you are satisfied with the fit of your bracelet.

Get it right!

Use my example to plan your length and bead placement. For a 7½ in. (19cm) long bracelet, subtract 1½ in. (3.3cm) for the brass circle plus 1 in. (2.5cm) for the clasp. This leaves two sections of 2½ in. (6.6cm) wire on either side for the beads.

RUBY PHEASANT EARRINGS

This project is designed to show just how versatile beading wire can be. While most styles of beaded earrings are crafted from metal wire, using beading wire offers you a lovely, low-cost alternative. The stem of a pheasant feather is quite durable and adds a dramatic, textural touch to an extra-long pair of lightweight earrings. Crimping a feather to a small section of strung beads offers you an endless array of earring possibilities.

Skill level ★ Approximate completion time: **30 minutes**

What you need

- 6 in. (16.5cm) pieces of 0.18 beading wire (x2)
- 2mm gold-filled crimp beads (x4)
- 3mm faceted vermeil beads (x4)
- 17mm faceted oblong ruby-colored acrylic beads (x2)
- 6 in. (16.5cm) pheasant feathers in black and iridescent green (x2)
- 22mm gold-filled or vermeil ear wires (x2)
- Wire cutters
- Crimping pliers
- Chain-nose pliers

Get it right!

Prepare the feathers ahead of time by stripping the end strands from the main shaft of each one. You will need approximately 1½ in. (4cm) of stripped feather to string and crimp a 17mm bead. Hold the two feathers side by side and trim off the ends to make an even pair.

Assembling

Tie a loose overhand knot at one end of a piece of beading wire.

String the wire as follows: One crimp bead, one faceted vermeil bead, one ruby-colored acrylic bead, one faceted vermeil, and one crimp bead.

Knot the opposite end of the beading wire loosely to keep the beads from falling off.

Repeat the process with the second length of beading wire.

Slide a prepared feather stem into the holes of each bead grouping, making sure that the loosely tied knot is at back of the feather each time.

Use the wire cutters to trim off any feather stem that shows at the top of the bead groupings (see Fig. 1).

Fig. 1

Crimping

Crimp the crimp bead nearest the feather, with the feather stem inside the crimp bead (see "Crimping" on page 20).

Trim away the loose knot with your wire cutters, pushing the wire away from the feather stem to prevent accidently cutting off the feather.

At the opposite end of your bead wire, untie the knot and thread the wire back through the crimping bead to form a loop. Pull tight with your chain-nose pliers, keeping the loop at just 2–4mm long.

Crimp the top crimp bead and trim away the excess beading wire.

Finishing

Use the chain-nose pliers to pull open the bottom loop of one ear wire slightly (see Fig. 2).

Hook the top loop of a feathered earring onto the ear wire and press the loop closed again, with chain-nose pliers.

Repeat with the second ear wire.

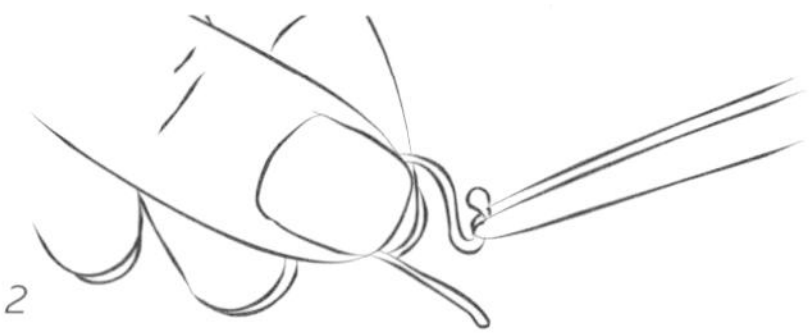

Fig. 2

TIERED FESTIVAL NECKLACE

This design demonstrates how you can use even the smallest, simplest of beads to make a fabulous, inexpensive, eye-catching accessory. With a little patience and good working light, you can string these six strands of faceted, gold-plated micro-seed beads in the course of two 1½-hour movies! You create the dramatic, tiered effect by assembling progressively longer strands of beads to a three-strand clasp.

Skill level ★ Approximate completion time: **3 hours**

What you need

- 30 in. (76cm) pieces of 0.18 beading wire (x6)
- One hank size 12/0 gold-plated faceted seed beads (approx. 12 temporarily strung strands)
- 20mm vermeil three-strand flower clasp with jump rings attached
- 2mm gold-filled crimp beads (x12)
- Flat ruler
- Chain-nose pliers
- Crimping pliers
- Wire cutters

Get it right!

To keep yourself from getting tangled while crimping the 12 crimps, work on stringing and crimping one strand of beads at a time.

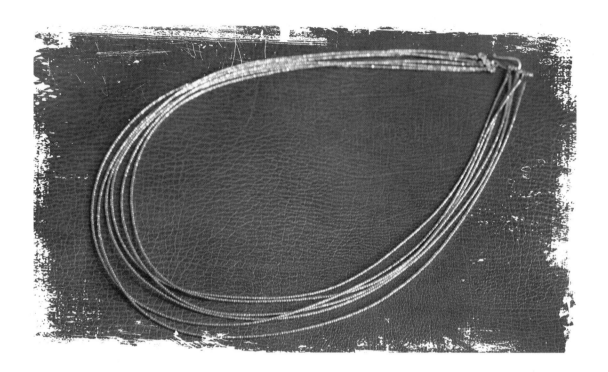

Stringing

The necklace shown measures 25 in. (63.5cm).

Knot one end of each of the six pieces of beading wire and begin stringing the tiny seed beads, using the following measurements:

First strand: String the beads up to 24 in. (61cm).

Second strand: String the beads up to 23½ in. (59.75cm).

Third strand: String the beads up to 23 in. (58.5cm).

Fourth strand: String the beads up to 22½ in. (57.25cm).

Fifth strand: String the beads up to 22 in. (56cm).

Sixth strand: String the beads up to 21½ in. (54.75cm).

Double-check the strand measurements by holding them tight against a flat ruler.

Crimping

With the male part of the clasp (the hook) pointing left, crimp your first strand onto the top jump rings either side of the three-strand clasp (see Fig. 1, and "Crimping" on page 20).

Fig. 1

Now crimp your second strand onto the same jump rings.

Crimp the third and fourth strands onto the middle jump rings of the clasp, and crimp the fifth and sixth strands onto the bottom jump rings either side of the clasp. Trim away any excess wire.

Variation

Try stringing a three-strand bracelet with spaced garnets. This sparkling piece is stunning when caught by the light, the garnets complementing the gold of the seed beads with their rich wine color. The design can be varied easily using different sizes and types of beads. Go larger for a bold, vibrant look or keep the scale delicate and elegant with tiny seed beads.

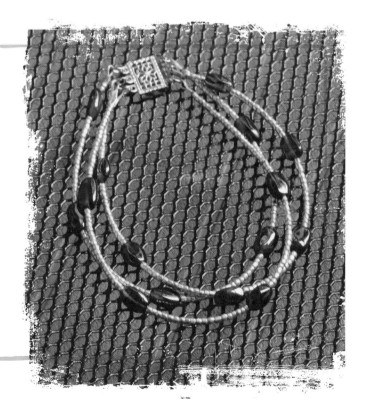

KNOTTING

CHAPTER 3

Knotting is another great technique to use for making jewelry and is easy to get to grips with. This particular stringing style offers protection from wear and tear on softer beads as well as a classic, clean look. Traditionally used for stringing pearls, due to their porous, delicate nature, any bead can be knotted if careful attention is paid to the size of the hole in the bead and the proper cord size is used. The projects featured here show how to use knotting to showcase your beaded jewelry in a contemporary style.

The Jewelry

Starting with a large-bead design, the Celadon Classic Bracelet allows you to use thicker cord, which is easy to unknot if you make a mistake while getting used to the technique. The Waterfall Earrings and Sea Breeze Necklace show just how versatile knotting can be when using pretty-colored cord to add contrast to the design. The delicate Summer's End Anklet uses spaced-out beads for an easy, open knotted style, while the Iced Coffee Necklace is an extra-long piece to try once you have the technique perfected. Finally, the Beachcomber Bracelet uses pretty little Bali silver spacers to add sparkle between the beads. In no time at all your knotted jewelry will have an evenly spaced, professional look with a sleek, stylish craftsmanship that will amaze your most savvy of friends.

CELADON CLASSIC BRACELET

With its large-sized, pretty glass pearls in pale colors and the most charming Hill Tribe fine silver flower clasp, this is the perfect bracelet to have on hand for luncheon dates. The beads chosen for this project have larger-sized holes at 2mm, which require the use of thicker cord. Focus on each knot as you slide it into place with the awl.

Skill level ★ Approximate completion time: **1 hour**

What you need

- Bead cord No.6 in gray
- Sterling-silver bead tips (x2)
- 10mm celadon glass pearls (x7)
- 12mm white glass pearls (x6)
- 20mm "S" clasp with Hill Tribe flower in fine silver
- 6mm sterling-silver jump rings (x2)

- Flexible measuring tape
- Bead board
- Scissors
- Awl
- Jeweler's cement
- Chain-nose pliers

Measuring

Measure your wrist for the completed piece using the flexible measuring tape (see "Measuring Up" on page 19).

The piece shown measures 8 in. (20cm).

Lay out your beads on the bead board, from the clasp outward, allowing ⅛ in. (2–3mm) between each one for knotting.

Get it right!

The larger the beads, the more width you should add to your bracelet length. For example, the beads used in this project added ½ in. (12mm) to the overall length needed to knot a comfortable bracelet. This is because the larger beads stand off the wrist, making the circumference that much larger.

You can avoid making too small a bracelet with larger beads by adding ½–¾ in. (12mm–18mm) to your final measurement. Check the bracelet often on your wrist as you near the end of stringing the beads in your design.

Knotting

Unravel the bead cord and make a double knot at one end.

Slide on a bead tip, with the open side facing out and knot the cord again (see "Knotting" on page 22).

With this done, you can string and knot each bead. Each time, use the awl to help get the knot as close to the bead as possible. The beads should be be strung alternately, starting and ending with a celadon pearl.

Once you have reached your final measurement, check the size of your bracelet by holding it up to your wrist.

Make sure to accommodate for the size of the clasp: There should be enough give that you can clasp the bracelet by yourself.

String on a bead tip, open side facing out, and tie a double knot inside the open clamshell (see Fig. 1).

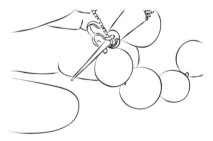

Fig. 1

Dot each double knot with jeweler's cement and trim the cord. Press the clamshell part of each bead tip closed using chain-nose pliers (see Fig. 2).

Fig. 2

Finishing

Open each of the jump rings using chain-nose pliers (see "Opening and Closing Jump Rings" on page 22), hook a bead tip onto each, and slide the jump rings onto the clasp.

Press them closed with chain-nose pliers to complete the piece (see Fig. 3).

Fig. 3

Variation

Try knotting other materials, such as a ribbon, between the beads for a different look. This bracelet has a gorgeous, olive-green silk ribbon knotted between different-shaped moss agate stone beads. Tie the ends of the ribbon to the clasp and add a drop of jeweler's cement to keep them from unraveling.

WATERFALL EARRINGS

Dripping with sparkling beads in a mix of shapes, sizes, and colors, these earrings are made up of a wonderful selection of miscellaneous beads. These were left over from other projects, but you could also have a great time sourcing them especially from your favorite suppliers.

These earrings will take anywhere from 1–2 hours to complete, but they are straightforward to make.

Skill level ★ Approximate completion time: **1–2 hours**

What you need

- Bead cord No.4 in light blue
- 10mm Swarovski crystal teardrop beads (x4)
- 7mm blue quartz stone chips (x4)
- 6mm white-and-clear swirled Givre glass beads (x4)
- 4mm clear quartz rectangle beads (x4)
- 18mm sterling-silver Bali twist rings (x2)
- 6mm faceted clear quartz beads (x4)
- 5mm freshwater button pearls (x4)

- 10mm green satin glass tubes (x4)
- 5mm frosted green rice beads (x2)
- 4mm pastel green glass beads (x2)
- 4mm clear glass beads (x2)
- 18mm sterling-silver ear wires (x2)
- Awl
- Scissors
- Jeweler's cement
- Chain-nose pliers

Get it right!

Take the time to set the beads up on the bead board, arranging and rearranging until you have a pleasing design that flows from one strand to the next.

Knotting

Unwind the bead cord and tie a double knot near one end.

String the following beads, knotting between each one (see "Knotting" on page 22): One Swarovski crystal teardrop, one blue quartz stone chip, one white-and-clear swirled Givre bead, and one clear quartz rectangle.

Use a double knot to tie the strand of four beads onto a silver Bali twist ring, without cutting the bead cord.

Now tie a knot in the dangling cord, close to the silver Bali twist ring, and slide on the following beads, knotting between each one: one faceted clear quartz, one freshwater button pearl, one green satin tube, and one faceted clear quartz.

Cut the cord approximately ½ in. (12mm) from the last knot.

Start a third strand of beads by tying a double knot at the end of the cord.

String on the following beads, knotting between each one: one frosted green rice bead, one freshwater button pearl, one pastel green glass bead, one white-and-clear swirled Givre glass, and one quartz rectangle (see Fig. 1).

Fig. 1

Use a double knot to tie the strand of four beads onto the silver Bali twist ring, without cutting the cord (see Fig. 2).

Fig. 2

Now tie a knot in the dangling cord, close to the silver Bali twist ring, and slide on the following beads, knotting between each one: one clear glass bead, one green satin tube, one blue quartz stone chip, and one crystal teardrop.

Tie a double knot after the last bead and cut the cord.

Repeat these steps to make the second earring.

Once you have strung both earrings, dot a drop of jeweler's cement on each of the end knots that you have made, and on the knots on the twisted silver rings. Leave them for about 15–20 minutes for the cement to dry.

Finishing

To complete each earring, take an ear wire, and gently open its loop using chain-nose pliers—just enough to thread the brass Bali twist ring onto the loop. Then use the chain-nose pliers to press the loop closed again (see Fig. 3).

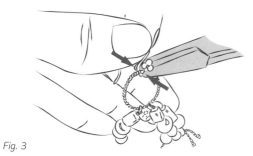

Fig. 3

SEA BREEZE NECKLACE

Breathtaking in its simplicity, this freshwater-pearl necklace features a frosted sea foam glass flower that is set off beautifully by the pale green pearls and green cord. It measures 21 in. (53cm)—a perfect length for a wide scoop-neck summer blouse. You will love the way this necklace drapes.

Skill level ★ Approximate completion time: **2–3 hours**

What you need

- Bead cord No.4 in peridot green
- Sterling-silver bead tips (x2)
- 15 in. (38cm) strand of 7mm pastel-green freshwater pearls
- 30mm matte sea-foam glass flower
- 2 in. (5cm) sterling-silver flower-tipped head pin
- Hill Tribe silver toggle clasp with jump rings attached
- Flexible measuring tape
- Bead board
- Awl
- Half-round-nose pliers
- Flush cutters
- Jeweler's cement
- Scissors
- Chain-nose pliers

Get it right!

To create the asymmetrical look this piece has, measure where you would like your flower to lie. For example, in the necklace shown, the flower is approximately 8½ in. (22cm) from the clasp at the back of the neck. To achieve this, lay the flower on the bead board and divide the pearls so that the first 12 in. (30cm) before the flower is filled with pearls, with the remaining pearls coming after the flower.

Measuring

Measure for your completed piece using the flexible measuring tape (see "Measuring Up" on page 19).

The necklace shown measures 21 in. (53cm).

Set up your pearls on the bead board so that 26 pearls are to one side of the flower and 40 pearls are to the other side.

Unwind the bead cord and tie a double knot near the end that is not attached to the needle.

Knotting

Slide on one of the bead tips, with the open side facing outward, and knot the cord after it (see "Knotting" on page 22).

Begin stringing the pearls, knotting after each one.

If you want more color from the cord to show between each bead, use double knots.

When you have strung and knotted the first 26 pearls, set your necklace down and begin wire-wrapping a bail for your glass flower. Do this by sliding the flower face down onto a flower-tipped head pin.

Use half-round-nose pliers to form a loop in the head pin wire and wrap the wire two or three times around the loop to secure it (see "Wire Wrapping" on page 24).

Cut off the extra wire using flush cutters (see Fig. 1).

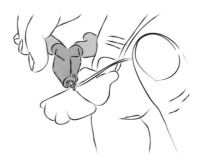

Fig. 1

Slide the flower onto the strand of knotted pearls and tie a double knot after it (see Fig. 2).

Fig. 2

Now return to the pearls, stringing and knotting again until you have used them all up.

Tie a double knot in the cord, slide on the second bead tip, with the open side facing outward, and tie another double knot.

Place drops of jeweler's cement on each knot inside the bead tips.

Cut the cord.

Finishing

Use chain-nose pliers to press the bead tips closed.

Now attach the hooks of the bead tips to the jump rings on the toggle clasp, using chain-nose pliers to gently open and close the jump rings (see "Opening and Closing Jump Rings" on page 22).

SUMMER'S END ANKLET

The design for this anklet gives you another unique way to use knotting for your handmade jewelry. The tiny, delicate beads and silver charms add bits of sparkle throughout the piece while a lovely, fine-silver flower dangles in the center. The technique used—spacing the beads on colored cord—works well with any type of jewelry, including necklaces and bracelets.

Skill level ★ ★ Approximate completion time: **1 hour**

What you need

- Bead cord No.4 in blue
- Bead cord No.4 in green
- Sterling-silver bead tips (x2)
- 2mm blue/green aventurine stone beads (x18)
- 2mm sterling-silver charm dangles (x6)
- 4mm light Vitrail-colored Swarovski crystal bicones (x6)
- 8mm Hill Tribe fine-silver flower charm

- 7mm sterling-silver jump ring
- 12mm sterling silver lobster-claw clasp, with jump rings attached
- Flexible measuring tape
- Awl
- Scissors
- Jeweler's cement
- Chain-nose pliers

Measuring

Measure for your completed piece using the flexible measuring tape (see "Measuring Up" on page 19).

The piece shown measures 9 in. (23cm)—the average size of an adult woman's ankle.

Knotting

Unwind both strands of cord and knot them together near one end, using a double knot.

Slide a bead tip onto both cords with the open side facing outward, and knot the cords again (see "Knotting" on page 22).

The beads are strung and knotted in an alternating pattern.

Starting with the green cord, use the awl to place a knot approximately ½ in. (1.25cm) from the bead tip.

String one aventurine bead, one silver charm, and then one aventurine. Knot again.

Now measure 1 in. (2.5cm) from the your last knot on the green cord, and tie a knot at this spot in the blue cord.

String one aventurine, one crystal, then one aventurine onto the blue cord. Knot again.

To keep these two strands together, tie an overhand knot in them.

Now measure 1 in. (2.5cm) from the overhand knot and tie a knot at this point on the green cord. String one aventurine, one crystal, then one aventurine onto the green cord. Knot again.

About ¼ in. (1cm) along from the last knot on the green cord, tie a knot in the blue cord. String one aventurine bead, one silver charm, and then one aventurine. Knot again.

At around 4 in. (10cm) along your anklet measurement—roughly halfway—tie a knot in the blue cord and string one aventurine, one silver charm, and one aventurine. Knot again.

Knot the green cord just below the last knot of the blue cord and string one crystal, the silver flower charm, and one more crystal. Knot again.

Use the needle from the blue cord to push the cord through the crystal, charm, crystal grouping you have just completed on the green cord, bringing both cords together.

If you have trouble pushing the needle through the crystals, use chain-nose pliers to manipulate the needle and to pull the tip of the needle from the other side of the beads (see Fig. 1).

Fig. 1

Repeat the groupings from the first half of the anklet on the second half, taking care to measure out properly and to use the awl to place the knots.

Double-knot the two cords at the end of the anklet, and thread on the second bead tip.

Double-knot again and trim.

Finishing

Apply a drop of jeweler's cement to the knots in both bead tips.

Use chain-nose pliers to gently open the jump rings attached to the clasp (see "Opening and Closing Jump Rings" on page 22).

Hook a bead tip into each, and close them again.

ICED COFFEE NECKLACE

With creamy barrel beads and liquid smoky quartz ovals, this piece has a distinct coffee look to it! The dramatic necklace is inspired by jewelry designer Stephanie Gibson's extra-long, versatile, knotted creations that give wearers two lovely options—either to wear them doubled up, choker style, or dramatically draped, princess style. At 32 in. (81cm), this necklace will take a while to string, so give yourself a full afternoon of leisure time to complete the piece.

Skill level ★ Approximate completion time: **4–5 hours**

What you need

- Bead cord No.6 in brown or black
- Sterling-silver bead tips (x2)
- 10mm howlite stone barrel beads (x48)
- 2mm sterling-silver spacers (x18)
- 15mm smoky quartz ovals (x9)
- 20mm sterling-silver Bali "S" clasp with jump rings attached
- Flexible measuring tape
- Bead board
- Awl
- Jeweler's cement
- Scissors
- Chain-nose pliers

Get it right!

To make knotting easier on your fingers during this long project, try gripping the cord with a pair of fine-point chain-nose pliers instead of using the awl. Still with the cord gripped in the pliers, use tweezers to push the knot as close to the bead as you can. Then slide the pliers out of the knot and close them again over the cord, right above the knot, and use the tip of the pliers to slide the knot into a tightened position.

Measuring

Measure for your completed piece using the flexible measuring tape (see "Measuring Up" on page 19).

The necklace shown measures 32 in. (81cm).

Lay out your beads on the bead board, from the clasp outward, allowing ⅛ in. (2–3mm) between each one for knotting.

Knotting

Unwind the bead cord and tie a double knot near one end. Slide on a bead tip, with the open side facing out. Knot the cord again (see "Knotting" on page 22).

String 18 of the howlite stone barrel beads, knotting after each one.

Use the following pattern for stringing the smoky quartz ovals: Tie a knot; string one silver spacer, one smoky quartz oval, and one silver spacer. This keeps the knots from sliding into the larger holes of the smoky quartz ovals. Repeat the pattern for all nine smoky quartz ovals and 18 silver spacers (see Fig. 1), ending the sequence with a knot.

Fig. 1

Finishing

Continue stringing the howlite beads, knotting after each one.

Once you have used the remaining 30 beads, double-knot the cord, slide on a bead tip, and double-knot the cord again.

Set all of the knots with jeweler's cement and trim the cord. Then close the bead tips using chain-nose pliers.

Use chain-nose pliers to gently open the jump rings attached to the clasp (see "Opening and Closing Jump Rings" on page 22), hook a bead tip into each, and close them again (see Fig. 2).

Fig. 2

BEACHCOMBER BRACELET

Inspired by long walks on the beach, this bracelet incorporates the taupe color of sand, a hint of brown for driftwood, rocks tumbled smooth and bleached white from the sun, and the treasured find of iridescent sea glass. The beads and findings were chosen not just for the monochromatic color scheme, but also for their mix of sizes. You can keep the weight of the bracelet balanced by alternating small beads with large ones.

Skill level ★ Approximate completion time: **45 minutes**

What you need

- 4–5mm Bali silver daisy, star, twist, and wheel spacers (x18)
- 3mm corrugated sterling silver beads (x2)
- 30mm magnesite stone
- 10mm iridescent glass bead
- 6mm brown clay tube bead
- 20mm faceted wooden bead
- 13mm carved acrylic coin bead
- 12mm Bali silver-filigree bead
- 12mm brown clay disc bead
- 6mm mother-of-pearl bead

- 18mm moonstone nugget bead
- Sterling-silver bead tips (x2)
- 15mm sterling-silver Bali "S" clasp with jump rings attached
- Bead cord No.4 in blue, green, or off-white
- Flexible measuring tape
- Bead board
- Awl
- Jeweler's cement
- Scissors
- Chain-nose pliers

Measuring

Measure your wrist for the completed piece using the flexible measuring tape (see "Measuring Up" on page 19). The bracelet shown measures 7½ in. (19cm) in length.

Designing

Lay out your beads on the bead board, from the clasp outward, allowing ⅛ in. (2–3mm) between each one for knotting. For this bracelet the design was as follows: Knot, Bali daisy, large magnesite stone, Bali daisy, knot, Bali daisy, iridescent glass bead, Bali daisy, knot, Bali star, small brown clay tube bead, Bali star, knot, Bali twist, faceted wooden bead, Bali twist, knot, carved acrylic coin bead, knot, Bali daisy, Bali silver-filigree bead, Bali daisy,

---

Get it right!

When measuring for your bracelet, you need to take into account the clasp and the bead tips. Added together, this will come to approximately 1¼ in. (2.5cm). The combined length of beads needed for the bracelet therefore needs to be approximately 6¼ in. (16.5cm).

---

knot, corrugated bead, Bali star, brown clay disc bead, Bali star, corrugated bead, knot, Bali daisy, Bali wheel bead, mother-of-pearl bead, Bali wheel bead, Bali daisy, knot, Bali star, moonstone nugget bead, Bali star, and a final knot.

Knotting

Unwind the bead cord and tie a double knot near one end. Slide on a bead tip with the open side facing out. Tie another knot right after the bead tip, using the awl to guide it into place and tightening it with your fingers (see "Knotting" on page 22).

String and knot your beads, following the order of your arrangement on the bead board. Because all the beads on this piece are different, be sure to pay careful attention to the sizes of the holes. Check each bead after sliding it onto the bead cord to make sure it does not slide over the last knot you made. If it does, remove the bead and tie a second knot on top of the first; this will add bulk to the knot (see Fig. 1).

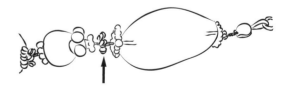

Fig. 1

Checking

Once all the beads have been strung and knotted on the bead cord, check the measurement by holding it up to the bead board and your wrist. Add any beads necessary to make the bracelet longer before finishing.

Finishing

Once you are satisfied with the final measurement of the bracelet, tie a knot after the last bead, slide on the bead tip, and tie a double knot. Apply a

drop of jeweler's cement to the knots in both the bead tips and close them with the chain-nose pliers. Trim away the excess bead cord from both sides. Attach the hooks of the bead tips to the jump rings on both sides of the clasp, closing them with the chain-nose pliers (see Fig. 2 and "Opening and Closing Jump Rings" on page 22).

Fig. 2

WIRE WRAPPING
CHAPTER 4

E asily the most versatile technique in jewelry making, you can use wire wrapping to create dangling charms and wire-wrap bead links, to incorporate custom lengths of chain and filigree into your designs, to wire-wrap beaded rings, and to attach clasps using jump rings.

The Jewelry

Vintage lockets, watches, keys, and other bits can all be attached securely using wire wrapping. Whimsy Locket makes an old locket look new by rubbing a coat of fresh aqua-colored acrylic paint into its surface. Wire-wrapped to an eclectic bunch of beads, it really makes for an eye-catching piece.

And don't be afraid to mix old with new. There are vintage suppliers in abundance, whose wonderful, individual components will make your designs even more unique. Floral Filigree Earrings does just this, pairing modern, faceted chalcedony with fancy filigree flowers, hung from vermeil ear wires. These same chalcedony briolette beads would look amazing wire-wrapped to large hoops as dangles. In the Bird's Nest Necklace, three freshwater pearls nestle inside an elegant sterling-silver wire-wrapped nest.

The Sugared Rose Ring makes good use of a yummy looking carved candy-jade rose, while the Turquoise Garden Necklace is an asymmetrical, beaded link necklace that features an assembled acrylic and brass filigree flower. The Orange Blossom Bracelet uses wire wrapping to hold together lots of little pieces of chain—this is such a popular and fashionable nostalgic look. Finally, the Enameled Floral Necklace uses a stack of funky flowers for colorful retro style. Once you have mastered a smooth, tight wire wrap, there is nothing in the way of you creating pieces that will attract attention wherever you go!

WHIMSY LOCKET

A charming brass locket hangs amid a mix of dangling beads from a large-patterned designer chain. You can create this look with any locket and customize its fit by lengthening or shortening the chain piece. The "whimsy" comes from the lovely mix of contrasting colors and textures.

Skill level ★ Approximate completion time: **30 minutes**

What you need

- 7mm brass jump rings (x2)
- 29 in. (73.5cm) length of patterned brass chain
- 16mm brass lobster-claw clasp
- 3 in. (7.5cm) length of brass wire
- Brass embossed or filigree locket
- 2mm pearls (x2) (to keep the large fuchsia bead in place)
- Brass bead caps (x2)
- 17mm fuchsia acrylic moon-glow bead
- 4–7mm mixed beads (x5) (this necklace uses one pink jade star, one matte-purple glass round, one olive acrylic moon-glow, one turquoise glass round, and one cloisonné oval bead)

- 2 in. (5.8cm) brass headpins (x5)
- Chain-nose pliers (2 pairs)
- Half-round-nose pliers
- Turquoise acrylic paint
- Paper towel
- Flush cutters

Assembling

The necklace shown measures 30 in. (76cm).

Use two pairs of chain-nose pliers to open one of the jump rings (see "Opening and Closing Jump Rings" on page 22) and hook it through the last link of the brass chain and also through the attachment loop of the lobster-claw clasp.

Close the jump ring. Attach the second jump ring to the opposite end of the chain in the same way.

Take the piece of brass wire and use the half-round-nose pliers to form a loop approximately ¾ in. (2cm) up from one end of the wire, thread this through the hanging loop on the locket (see "Wire Wrapping" on page 24).

Now wire-wrap the short end of the brass wire around the longer end, just two or three times, in order to attach the locket securely.

Slide the following onto the brass wire: One pearl, one brass bead cap, the acrylic moon-glow bead, one brass bead cap, and one pearl (see Fig. 1).

Form another loop in the brass wire, using the half-round-nose pliers.

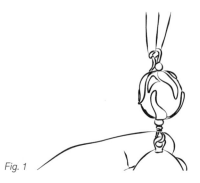

Fig. 1

Find the middle link of your assembled necklace chain by holding it up by the clasp, and thread the wire loop through the link of your beaded locket attachment.

Now wire-wrap the loop until a tight spiral has formed and the locket is securely attached to the chain.

Finishing

To complete the necklace, slide each of the mixed beads onto brass headpins and wire-wrap, one by one, onto the top loop of the beaded locket attachment (see Fig. 2).

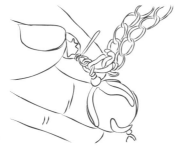

Fig. 2

Place a pea-sized drop of acrylic paint onto a piece of paper towel and rub over the brass.

Wait a few seconds and rub again with a clean section of the paper towel.

This removes the paint from the surface of the brass but leaves the color in the crevices of the embossed design (see Fig. 3).

Fig. 3

FLORAL FILIGREE EARRINGS

These fanciful brass-filigree earrings feature rhinestones and faceted lime chalcedony briolette beads. Their large size is barely felt owing to the lightweight nature of the open filigree and the glamorous look of the pair is enhanced by the delicate wire-wrapped, precious stones.

Skill level ★ Approximate completion time: **30 minutes**

What you need

- 12 in. (30.5cm) pieces of 28-gauge dead-soft gold-filled wire (x2)
- 10mm lime chalcedony briolettes (x2)
- 40mm brass-filigree flowers (x2)
- 20mm gold-filled ear wires with ball tips (x2)
- 5mm pointed-back crystal rhinestones (x2)

- Half-round-nose pliers
- Chain-nose pliers (2 pairs)
- Jeweler's cement
- Flush cutters

Assembling

Take one piece of gold-filled wire and find its center, creasing it slightly. Do not bend the wire at this stage.

Slide on one of the faceted chalcedony briolettes and bend the wire now, centering the briolette in the middle (see Fig. 1).

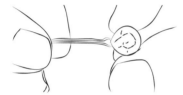

Fig. 1

Use the half-round-nose pliers to form a loop 2mm above the briolette tip in the, now doubled, wire (see "Wire Wrapping" on page 24).

Thread the double wire through one of the petals in the filigree flower so that the loop sits at the tip of the flower (see Fig. 2).

Fig. 2

Use the chain-nose pliers in one hand to grip the doubled wire loop against the filigree and use your other hand to wire-wrap the gold-filled wire, in a spiral, around the doubled wire and down to the tip of the briolette.

Keep a firm grip on the pliers and good tension on the doubled wire as you wrap, gently pulling until the tip of the briolette is covered and the wire wrapping measures ⅛ in. (3–4mm) wide.

Begin to wind the wire back up to the beginning loop, using the second set of chain-nose pliers to press the wrap into place.

Get it right!

Chalcedony is a gorgeous stone, prized for its glowing opaque appearance. When cut into a faceted briolette, the drill holes can be quite tiny and difficult to fit wire through. For this reason, it is best to work with the thinnest gauge gold-filled wire, 28- or 30-gauge thickness. Wrapping a briolette may seem awkward at first, so try practicing with a thin, inexpensive brass or steel wire and durable acrylic teardrop beads until you feel comfortable forming wire wraps with the more delicate gold-filled wire.

Once you have reached the filigree, push the doubled wire through the same point that you threaded the first wire loop.

Push the doubled wire through to the back of the filigree. Cut off any excess wire using the flush cutters and press the cut ends into the wire wrap with the chain-nose pliers so there are no sharp ends poking out.

Finishing

Use chain-nose pliers to open the end loop of the ball-tip ear wires and thread the ear wire through the top petal of the filigree flower.

Now press the loop closed using chain-nose pliers so that the filigree does not fall off the ear wire.

Touch a drop of jeweler's cement to the center hole of the filigree flower and set one of your rhinestones in place.

Make the second earring in exactly the same way, then lie the flowers flat for 20–30 minutes to allow the cement to harden.

Variation

Once you have practiced the briolette wrapping technique, try wrapping briolettes as dangles onto different shapes and styles of brass components. The earring variation shown has a sunset orange chalcedony wire-wrapped to a hammered brass ring.

BIRD'S NEST NECKLACE

A miniature replica of a bird's nest in silver wire! Darling in its simplicity, this little nest with three pearl eggs is so easy to recreate you will not want to stop at just one. Make two for a pair of earrings or several linked together for a bracelet.

Skill level ★ Approximate completion time: **30 minutes**

What you need

- 5mm oval cream or white freshwater pearls (x3)
- 4 ft. (120cm) of 24-gauge dead-soft sterling-silver wire
- 4mm jump ring in the same wire type
- 16 in. (40cm) necklace chain, with clasp
- Half-round-nose pliers
- Chain-nose pliers
- Flush cutters

Get it right!

The nest shown is made with a 24-gauge wire, which will fit into inner holes of most 5–6mm freshwater pearls. As with any wire-wrapping technique you are trying for the first time, practice using a less expensive copper or brass before completing in sterling-silver or gold-filled wire.

The Eggs

Slide the three freshwater pearls onto the wire leaving approximately 1 in. (2.5cm) at one end. Twist the two wires together once or twice to keep the pearls in place. Form the short end of the wire into a neat circle at the back of 'the pearls (see Fig. 1).

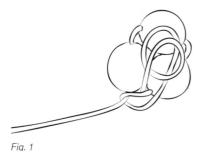

Fig. 1

The Nest

Use the long end of the wire to form the nest, wrapping it loosely around the pearls in circles. These do not need to be perfect. Keep going until you have approximately 10 in. (25cm) of wire left over.

Now thread the wire through the center of the "nest" circle between two of the pearls, up over the edge, and down again. Pull the wire tight as

you do this, so that it is snug against the wire nest. Repeat this twice between each pearl for a total of six times. You should end with 1–2 in. (2.5–5cm) of wire at the back (see Fig. 2).

Fig. 2

Finishing

Push the end of the remaining wire flat against the back of the nest and use the half-round-nose pliers to form a loop approximately ⅛ in. (3mm) above the top of the nest. Finish the wire-wrap using chain-nose pliers (see "Wire Wrapping" on page 24).

Open the jump ring using the chain-nose pliers (see "Opening and Closing Jump Rings" on page 22) and thread the wire-wrapped loop onto the jump ring. Now thread the jump ring onto the necklace chain and press it closed.

Variation

A wire-wrapped bird's nest can easily be turned into a ring by using an extra 12 in. (30cm) of the wire for the woven circles and shaping the ring base around a mandrel, (see the "Sugared Rose Ring" on page 88). To finish the piece off, simply thread the wire back into the bottom of the nest as you shape your wire ring, instead of forming a loop at the top as you did for the necklace.

SUGARED ROSE RING

This bright-pink, carved candy-jade rose has a flat bottom with a hole drilled from one side to the other, and so lends itself well to this wire-wrapping technique. However, any bead can be secured and shown off this way and will be secure enough for daily wear. Although the technique looks complex, wire-wrapped rings are so easy to master that you will soon find yourself making handfuls!

Skill level ★   Approximate completion time: **30 minutes**

What you need

- 18mm candy-jade carved rose with a side-to-side drilled hole
- 15–18 in. (38–46cm) piece of 20-gauge round half-hard, gold-filled wire
- Flexible measuring tape
- Ring mandrel
- Chain-nose pliers
- Flush cutters
- Jeweler's file or emery board

Get it right!

The trick to keeping your wire wrapping symmetrical and even is to work on one end of the wire and then switch to the other, moving back and forth wrapping just a few loops at a time. Use chain-nose pliers to shape your loops evenly around the base wire of the ring.

Measuring

Measure your finger using the flexible measuring tape (see "Measuring Up" on page 19).

Slide the carved rose to the center of your piece of wire and place it, bottom-side down, against the ring mandrel at one size larger than the measurement you just took. The wire wrapping will create a smaller sized ring so using a larger size on the ring mandrel will help compensate for this.

Take the two ends of the wire to the back of the mandrel and cross them over at the back.

Assembling

Holding the wire crossed at the back of the mandrel, pull the original right-hand wire around to the front of the mandrel and slide it underneath the back of the rose, all the way to the right side again.

Repeat this step with the original left-hand wire, sliding it underneath the back of the rose, and then bringing it back to the left-hand side (see Fig. 1).

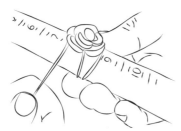

Fig. 1

Bend the wire that is now on the right upward so that it is perpendicular to the right-hand side of the rose.

Then bend the wire that is now on the left down instead of up, still perpendicular to the rose, on the left-hand side.

Slide the wire off the mandrel, keeping the crossed wires at the back together between your thumb and first finger (see Fig. 2).

Fig. 2

Don't worry if the ring looks sloppy and all wrong at this point, it will soon come together.

You will have formed a basic ring shape. The idea now, is to thread each length of wire through and around this ring a number of times, to wire-wrap it into shape.

Start on the left-hand side, threading the loose end wire through the center of the ring.

Pull the wire tight around the wires that make the basic ring shape, using chain-nose pliers to push the wrap up as close as you can to the rose.

Repeat twice more, then do the same thing with the right-hand wire (see Fig. 3).

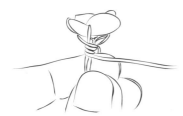

Fig. 3

Finishing

Continue wrapping each side of the ring in the same way, alternating left and right with every few wraps, and taking the time to push the wire up against the previous wrap and to tighten the loops using chain-nose pliers.

Once you have used up all the wire, trim away any excess using the flush cutters.

Use the jeweler's file to smooth down the cut edges of the wire so that there are no pointy edges to scratch the wearer.

TURQUOISE GARDEN NECKLACE

Lovely links of turquoise Lucite nuggets hang beautifully under an offset, assembled brass-filigree, acrylic, and rhinestone flower. Comfortable and lightweight, but ever so elegant, this piece is designed for everyday through evening wear. Delightful in its simple construction, you will love to customize this piece with your own choice of contrasting colors. Linking your beads together with wire wrapping is very easy; in fact the only difficult part is remembering to stop yourself from completing the wrap and inserting the previous bead link!

Skill level ★ ★ Approximate completion time: **1 hour**

What you need

- 12mm turquoise Lucite nugget beads (x10)
- 20 in. (51cm) piece of 24-gauge, dead-soft brass wire
- 25mm brass-filigree component
- 14 in. (35.5cm) piece of brass circle chain
- 6mm brass jump rings (x2)
- 10mm brass lobster-claw clasp
- 30mm translucent amber-brown acrylic flower finding
- 15mm turquoise three-petal acrylic flower
- 4mm pointed-back crystal rhinestone
- Flexible measuring tape
- Bead board
- Flush cutters

- Chain-nose pliers
- Half-round-nose pliers
- Epoxy

Get it right!

I like to leave a little bit of a tail in each wire wrap, going back later to tighten up any loose ones and trimming the extra wire away once I am satisfied with the spiral. This way you achieve a more consistent finish.

Measuring

Measure for your completed necklace using the flexible measuring tape (see "Measuring Up" on page 19).

Lay out your beads on the bead board, from the center of the design outward, leaving approximately ½ in. (1.25cm) between each bead to allow for wire wrapping.

The necklace shown measures 22 in. (56cm).

Assembling

Wire-wrap nine of the turquoise Lucite nuggets together, leaving the ends of the first and last beads unwrapped (see "Wire Wrapping" on page 24).

To do so, cut a 2 in. (5cm) piece of wire, form a loop approximately ¾ in. (2cm) from one end using half-round-nose pliers. Leave this unwrapped, and thread on your first bead.

Now form a loop at the opposite end of the wire and wire-wrap it.

Cut a second 2 in. (5cm) piece of wire, form a loop approximately ¾ in. (2cm) from one end and thread this through the wire-wrapped loop of the first bead, and wire-wrap it.

Thread on a second bead, form another loop, wire-wrap it, and so on until you have done all nine beads, remembering not to wrap the final loop.

Now thread one of the unwrapped ends of wire into the brass filigree, form a loop, and wrap it until securely attached to the strand of linked beads (see Fig. 1).

Fig. 1

At the opposite end of the strand, thread the unwrapped end of wire into one of the end links of the brass circle chain, form a loop, and wrap it until securely attached to the strand of linked beads.

Cut a 2 in. (5cm) piece of brass wire and wire-wrap your last Lucite bead to the free side of the brass filigree and to the end link at the opposite end of the brass circle chain (see Fig. 2).

Fig. 2

Finishing

Hold up the completed chain so that the beads are symmetrically aligned in the center. There should be one center bead with four beads on either side. Find the top link in the chain—you need to remove this in order to insert the clasp.

Pry open the links using chain-nose pliers, and attach the clasp by opening both jump rings, attaching them to the clasp, and then closing each on one end of the chain (see "Opening and Closing Jump Rings" on page 22).

To apply the acrylic flower pieces, place a pea-sized drop of epoxy onto the top of the amber flower finding, then press and hold the turquoise

three-petal flower on for 30 seconds until the glue sets. Add a drop of epoxy to the brass filigree, press, then hold your flowers into place for 30 seconds until the glue sets (see Fig. 3).

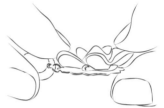

Fig. 3

Dab a tiny amount of epoxy onto the back of the rhinestone using a toothpick, and carefully press it into the centre of the flower cabochons. Leave the necklace flat to dry overnight.

ORANGE BLOSSOM BRACELET

This bohemian bracelet has a carefree, wildflower-type feel to it. It has been created using mismatched but complementary beads and charms in peach, orange, and apricot colors. They are asymmetrically spaced with bits of brass chain and a circle link, giving it a happy-go-lucky vibe that will cheer any wearer. Projects like this can be an enjoyable diversion from precise, complex designs that require a lot of focus and math figuring. Scour flea markets and yard sales for broken jewelry and single earrings. Treasures like these can easily be taken apart, cleaned up, and repurposed into personalized, contemporary pieces you will love to create and wear.

Skill level ★ ★   Approximate completion time: **1 hour**

What you need

- 6 in. (15cm) piece of 24-gauge, dead-soft brass wire
- 6mm brass jump rings (x2)
- 8mm faceted orange glass bead with aurora borealis coating
- 1½ in. (3.8cm) piece of brass Figaro chain and 1 in. (2.5cm) piece of brass Figaro chain
- 10mm peach acrylic flower with side-to-side top hole
- 1 in. (2.5cm) pieces of brass curb-link chain (x2)
- 6mm round orange crackle-glass bead
- 8mm brass circle link

- 8mm frosted apricot flat acrylic flower
- 1½ in. (3.8cm) brass head pins with ball tip (x2)
- 4mm orange stone bead
- 12mm peach acrylic three-petal flower
- Bendable brass leaf-patterned bead cap
- 12mm brass lobster-claw clasp
- Flexible measuring tape
- Bead board
- Half-round-nose pliers
- Chain-nose pliers (2 pairs)
- Flush cutters

Measuring

Measure for your completed bracelet using the flexible measuring tape (see "Measuring Up" on page 19).

Lay out your beads and chain on the bead board in your desired arrangement, working from the clasp backward.

Allow ¼ in. (5mm) between each bead for wire wrapping.

The bracelet shown measures 7 in. (17.5cm).

Assembling

Cut a 2 in. (5cm) piece of brass wire and form a loop approximately ¾ in. (2cm) from one end, using the half-round-nose pliers (see "Wire Wrapping" on page 24). Hook a jump ring onto the loop and wire-wrap the loop.

Slide on the faceted orange glass bead and form a second loop in the wire.

Thread the wire through the end link of the 1½ in. (3.8cm) piece of Figaro chain and wire-wrap the loop.

Cut another 2 in. (5cm) piece of brass wire and form a loop approximately ¾ in. (2cm) from one of the ends.

Thread the wire through the end link at the opposite end of the Figaro chain and wire-wrap the loop.

Slide on the peach acrylic flower with the side-to-side top hole and form a loop in the wire.

Thread the wire through the end link of both pieces of the brass curb-link chain and wire-wrap the loop (see Fig. 1).

Fig. 1

Cut another 2 in. (5cm) of brass wire and form a loop approximately ¾ in. (2cm) from one end using the half-round-nose pliers.

Thread the wire through the links at the opposite ends of the brass curb-link chain and wire-wrap the loop.

Slide on the orange crackle-glass bead and form a loop in the wire.

Wire-wrap this loop onto the brass circle link.

Slide the frosted apricot flat acrylic flower onto one of the ball-tip head pins. (If the head pin is too small, slide on a small seed bead to prevent the pin from slipping through the bead hole.)

Now form a loop in the head pin that will fit onto the brass circle link.

Wire-wrap the loop so that the flower dangles down from the brass ring.

Take the second brass head pin and slide on the orange stone bead, then the peach acrylic three-petal flower, and then the leaf-patterned bead cap.

Form a loop in the brass head pin.

Thread the head pin through the brass circle link and the last link of the 1 in. (2.5cm) piece of brass Figaro chain, and wire-wrap the loop (see Fig. 2).

Fig. 2

Finishing

All that is left to do is to attach the flower end of the bracelet to the lobster-claw clasp.

Open the second jump ring using two pairs of chain-nose pliers (see "Opening and Closing a Jump Ring" on page 22). Thread on the end link of the brass Figaro chain followed by the male end of the lobster-claw clasp (the hook end). Close the jump ring.

ENAMELED FLORAL NECKLACE

Treat yourself to a pop of color with this gorgeous, enameled layered-flower necklace. It makes for a fantastic summertime accessory. All you need is 30 minutes and a few metal components in addition to your new wire-wrapping skills to create this beautiful piece.

Skill level ⭐ Approximate completion time: **30 minutes**

What you need

- 5mm green-and-white striped glass bead
- 2 in. (5cm) antiqued brass head pin with ball tip
- 1 in. (2.5cm) black stamen enameled flower
- 1.8 in. (4.5cm) blue-gray enameled flower
- 2.5 in. (6cm) red daisy enameled flower
- 20mm antiqued brass bead cap
- 6mm antiqued brass jump rings (x3)

- 19 in. (48cm) antiquated brass chain
- 12mm antiqued brass lobster-claw clasp
- Half-round-nose pliers
- Flush cutters
- Chain-nose pliers (2 sets)
- Epoxy

Making the Flower

Slide the small green-and-white striped bead onto the headpin first. This will ensure that the larger-holed flower components do not slide off.

Slide the rest of the flower components onto the headpin in the order they fit best, the smallest first.

Slide on the brass bead cap face-side out to finish off the look in a more pleasing way (see Fig. 1).

Fig. 1

Wire Wrapping

Approximately ½ in. (1cm) from the base of your flower, form a loop in the head pin, using the half-round-nose pliers (see "Wire Wrapping" on page 24).

Continue wire-wrapping a spiral and tighten up the wrap with the chain-nose pliers. Cut off any extra wire with the flush cutters and press the cut end into the spiral.

Check to make sure the wire wrap is wider than the hole in the bead cap. If it is too small, the bead cap and flower components will slide backward on the headpin and become loose.

Push the wire wrap loop so that it lies flat against the back of the enameled flower with the loop opening close to what will be the top petal of the flower.

Attach a jump ring to the wire-wrapped loop (see "Opening and Closing Jump Rings" on page 22) and attach this to the center link of your brass chain (see Fig. 2).

Fig. 2

Finishing

Attach a jump ring to one side of the lobster-claw clasp, threading the end link of one side of the brass chain onto the same jump ring. Close the jump ring with chain-nose pliers.

Repeat this step with the other side of the chain and clasp.

Variation

Add a punch of color to your winter wardrobe with an enameled flower brooch. Add a drop of epoxy to the flat front of a brass pin back. Press it onto the back of the flower (under the wire-wrapped loop and position it so it does not show through the front petals of your brooch. Hold in place for 30 seconds so the epoxy sets. Now bend the wire-wrap, using the chain-nose pliers, so that it presses against the inside of the pin back. Let the epoxy set over night.

MIXED MEDIA
CHAPTER 5

Having mastered the techniques in the first four chapters of the book, now is the time to mix things up a bit to make truly unique and stylish jewelry that combines mixed media. This is all about thinking outside the box. This chapter also introduces the idea of creating your own ear wires, saving you money and giving you more options for personalized ear wire designs to complement your jewelry. Use these projects as inspiration and train yourself to look at any type of material and ask yourself how it can be incorporated into your own jewelry designs.

The Jewelry

The Swashbuckler Cuff features a stitched brass filigree as its focal point, set quite simply on grosgrain ribbon. The tiniest bit of bling makes for a charming pair of Felted Poppy Earrings, while the Delicate Posy Earrings show you how to combine cutout bits of crocheted lace with handmade ear wires together with a cute little wire spiral. In the Woodland Tendrils Bracelet, silk ribbons are knotted to a wire-wrapped jade bracelet with semi-precious stones as accents. Entwined Necklace uses different styles of glittering sterling-silver chains, decorated with mixed beads, to form a tumbling tasseled beauty.

Spiral Relic Earrings offers an artistic way to include coils of fabric with copper wire, and the Olivine Drape Necklace shows how to layer faceted crystals into a complex woven design.

SWASHBUCKLER CUFF

This bracelet was inspired by a cuff worn by a supermodel in a recent fashion magazine. The wide black ribbon and glint of brass filigree has just the right combination of modern boldness and antique flare, and is reminiscent of a rogue pirate with his ill-gotten gold filigree stitched flagrantly on his cuffed sleeve. The filigree for this project has been given a patina, as if it has been dredged from the sea.

Skill level ⭐ Approximate completion time: **30 minutes**

What you need

- 1½ x 2 in. (3.8 x 5cm) brass filigree stamping
- 8½ x 1½ in. (21.5 x 3.8cm) piece of black grosgrain ribbon
- Black cotton thread
- Decorative button for closure
- 2 in. (5cm) piece of black elastic cording
- 7½ x 1 in. (19 x 2.5cm) piece of black felt
- Dark green acrylic paint

- Turquoise acrylic paint
- Paper towel
- Flexible measuring tape
- Scissors
- Medium sewing needle
- Fabric glue

Preparing

Prepare the brass filigree ahead of time by adding a pea-sized drop of dark green acrylic paint to a piece of paper towel.

Rub the green paint all over the brass filigree and leave for just a few seconds.

Now rub over the brass again, this time with a clean section of the paper towel to remove the top layer of paint.

Repeat this with the turquoise paint, gently dabbing the paint on so that a little bit of the green paint shows through.

Once the paint has dried, buff the top of the brass filigree with a paper towel so that the gold color shines through.

Measuring

Measure your wrist using the flexible measuring tape, and determine the correct length for your cuff bracelet (see "Measuring Up" on page 19).

You want to cut the ribbon to accommodate the measured wrist size, plus 1 in. (2.5cm) for finishing the ends. The bracelet shown measures 7½ in. (19cm).

Assembling

Fold in and finger press ½ in. (1.25cm) hems to the wrong side at each end of the cut ribbon.

Cut 24 in. (60cm) of thread, thread the needle, and double-knot the ends together.

Use running stitch to baste the hem folds at both ends of the ribbon (see "Basic Stitch" on page 25).

Knot and cut off the excess thread.

Lay the ribbon flat, right side up, and center the filigree on top.

Using another piece of thread, and starting from the wrong side of the ribbon, sew up through the ribbon and over an open area in the brass filigree, then back down into the ribbon. Repeat this step at several points around the brass filigree to attach it securely to the right side of the ribbon (see Fig. 1).

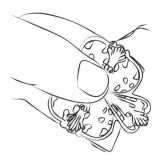

Fig. 1

Once all the points in the filigree have been attached to the ribbon, knot your thread securely on the wrong side and trim away the extra. Sew a decorative bead or button onto one hemmed end of the ribbon, right side up, and directly in the center (see Fig. 2).

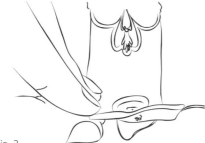

Fig. 2

At the opposite end, sew a loop of elastic thread that will stretch over the decorative button you just attached. This acts as a clasp for the ribbon cuff (see Fig. 3).

Fig. 3

Finishing

Attach the precut felt lining to your ribbon cuff, wrong sides together, using fabric glue.

Lay the bracelet flat and place a heavy weight on top while it dries—a big book will do.

Once the bracelet has dried, put it on and gently bend the filigree to the shape of your wrist.

FELTED POPPY EARRINGS

Who can resist the soft, rounded look of modern poppies crafted from felt? Whimsical and simple, you can craft these little flower earrings using lots of different colors and centers. Felt is a durable, but inexpensive, material that requires no hemming and therefore is ideal for a quick-and-easy sewing project. Add a bit of sparkle with some vintage sew-on crystals and these mod poppies are ready to wear!

Skill level ★ Approximate completion time: **30 minutes**

What you need

- 1 ¼ in. (3cm) black felt circles (x2)
- Black cotton thread
- 5mm crystal sew-on jewels (x2)
- 10mm silver-plated or sterling silver ear posts with glue on pads (x2)
- Medium needle
- Scissors
- Jeweler's cement
- Epoxy

Get it right!

Depending on the look you are after, you could use any number of decorative beads and embellishments. Try sewing seed beads in place of the rhinestones for a whimsical variation.

Preparing

Stretch and rub the felt circles between your fingers to remove as much of the loose lint as you can.

Assembling

Thread the needle with 24 in. (60cm) black thread and double-knot the ends together.

Bring the needle up through the back of one felt circle, at its center, through one corner of the sew-on crystal, and back down into the felt (see Fig. 1).

Fig. 1

Repeat for all four corners of the sew-on crystal, knotting the thread at the back of the felt circle.

On the back of the felt, make a small fold from the center to the edge and make small stitches to create a little dart on the wrong side of the fabric.

Repeat once or twice more round the circle. This will add a slight wave to the round circle, giving it more of a petal appearance (see Fig. 2).

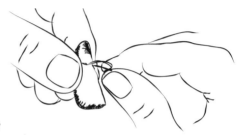

Fig. 2

To make certain the crystal centers do not come out of their settings, add a tiny drop of jeweler's cement beneath the crystal to keep it in place.

Repeat for the second felt circle.

Finishing

Drop some epoxy onto the flat pad at the front of the ear posts.

Press, then hold, the felt poppy to the ear post for a minute or so to ensure a tight bond.

Allow to set overnight.

DELICATE POSY EARRINGS

Flowers make a beautiful addition to many a jewelry project. These delicate crocheted lace flowers have an attractive antique look. Taken from a large crocheted piece, the flowers have been separated and layered, and then finished with wire-wrapped glass beads. Stay on the lookout for pieces of lace that can be cut apart and repurposed for your own handmade jewelry.

Skill level ★ Approximate completion time: **20 minutes**

What you need

- 1 in. (2.5cm) cream crocheted flowers (x2)
- ½ in. (10mm) pink crocheted flowers (x2)
- 5mm burgundy glass trumpet-flower beads (x2)
- 2 in. (5cm) 24-gauge copper headpins (x2)
- 1½ in. (3.8cm) pieces of 20-gauge copper wire (x2)
- Paintbrush
- Fabric glue
- Half-round-nose pliers
- Chain-nose pliers
- Wire-wrapping jig
- Flush cutters
- Jeweler's file or emery board

Get it right!

To make cutting your crocheted lace easier, steam-press the pieces first with an iron set on low to flatten them. Use the sharpest scissors possible to make clean cuts of the delicate threads.

Assembling

Using an inexpensive paintbrush, apply fabric glue to the middle of a large cream flower and press the small pink flower on top.

Let dry.

Slide a trumpet-flower bead onto a copper headpin and form a loop in the wire using the half-round-nose pliers (see "Wire Wrapping" on page 24).

Thread this loop through the bottom of the larger crocheted flowers and wire-wrap the loop, leaving ¾ in. (2cm) of wire pointed out to the side (see Fig. 1).

Fig. 2

Fig. 1

Grasp the end of the copper headpin with the chain-nose pliers and bend it in toward itself.

Now make a "swirl" with the end of the copper headpin: Grip the bent end so that it lies flat in the chain-nose pliers and push the end in toward itself again—you will need to adjust to grip with the pliers to complete the swirl (see Fig. 2).

Once the swirl is done, push it down so it lies flat against the trumpet-flower bead.

Finishing

Set up the wire-wrapping jig as shown, with a medium-sized peg above and to the right of the smaller peg.

Bend a piece of copper wire around the small peg, up between the two pegs, and around the medium peg to form an ear wire (see Fig. 3).

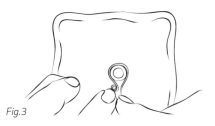

Fig.3

Use the flush cutters to cut the ear wire to the size you would like and file off the metal bur using the emery board.

Thread the open loop of the ear wire through the top petal of the crocheted cream flower and press closed using the chain-nose pliers.

Make the second earring in the same way.

WOODLAND TENDRILS BRACELET

Jade is such an earthy color of green, it gives a grounded look to most designs. Paired with fluffy crocheted pods, labradorite, moonstone, and tied silk ribbons, it turns into something a woodland elf might collect and treasure. Work in layers to achieve this look, wire-wrapping the stones and then the pods, finishing off with the silk ribbons. Add an ornate sterling silver Bali clasp to complete the look.

Skill level ★ Approximate completion time: **45 minutes**

What you need

- 12mm dark-green oval jade beads (x7)
- 14 in. (35.5cm) 24-gauge dead-soft sterling silver wire
- 1½ in. (3.8cm) sterling silver Bali "S" clasp with a set moonstone and jump rings attached
- 4mm faceted labradorite oval beads (x8)
- 1½ in. (3.8cm) sterling-silver head pins (x16)
- 5mm faceted moonstone rondell beads (x8)
- 2 in. (5cm) sterling silver head pins (x2)
- 4mm silver Bali flower beads (x2)

- 8mm flat rondell beads (x2)
- 1 in. (2.5cm) crocheted pod flowers (x2) (see Resources, page 141)
- 13mm silver filigree bead caps (x2)
- 32 in. (80cm) variegated olive-green silk ribbon
- Flexible measuring tape
- Bead board
- Half-round-nose pliers
- Chain-nose pliers
- Scissors

Measuring

Measure for your completed piece using the flexible measuring tape (see "Measuring Up" on page 19).

Deduct the clasp measurement from your wrist measurement to calculate how long the bead section needs to be.

For example, the bracelet shown measures 7½ in. (19cm) and the clasp measures 1½ in. (4cm) so the bead section needed to measure 6 in. (15cm) when wire-wrapped.

Lay out the necessary number of beads on the bead board, spacing them approximately ½ in. (1.25cm) apart to allow spacing for the wire-wrapped links.

Assembling

Begin your bracelet by wire-wrapping the jade ovals together, connecting them to the sterling silver Bali "S" clasp (see "Wire Wrapping" on page 24 and "Opening and Closing Jump Rings" on page 22).

Now add the labradorite beads to the bracelet by sliding each onto a 1½ in. (3.8cm) headpin and wire-wrapping one to each link between the jade ovals.

Repeat this with the moonstone beads, pairing them with the wire-wrapped labradorite (see Fig. 1).

Fig. 1

Using the 2 in. (5cm) headpins, string the following grouping on each: One Bali flower, one jade rondell, one crocheted pod flower, and one silver filigree bead cap.

Get it right!

You may find it easier to tie the silk ribbon into the wire-wrapped links by unclasping the bracelet, stretching it out to its full length, and pinning it with a safety pin to a tablecloth. This will keep it still and in place while you work your way down the bracelet with the silk ribbon pieces.

Wire-wrap each of these to the jump ring on the right-hand side of the Bali "S" clasp (see Fig. 2).

Fig. 2

Finishing

Cut 2 in. (5cm) pieces of variegated silk ribbon—16 in total—and tie one onto each link between the jade ovals (see Fig. 3).

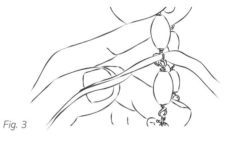

Fig. 3

Double-knot each silk ribbon and cut a V shape at each end. You can do this by folding the ribbon in half lengthwise and cutting at an angle from the open edge to the fold.

ENTWINED NECKLACE

This necklace has been crafted from a mix of sterling-silver chains, both bright and oxidized, with an eclectic array of beads: crystals, stone, glass, and pearl in rosy pink, purple, green, brick red, and copper, tumbling down a tassel of silver chain. Inexpensive, fine, sterling-silver chains can be built up to resemble a hefty piece when attached together using wire-wrapping. The tassel contains treasures collected over time that are purposefully random in their arrangement. Once the necklace chain pieces have been cut, you can enjoy the process of assembling the beads and chains to bring the collection together in front.

Skill level ★ ★ Approximate completion time: **1 hour**

What you need

- 10 in. (26cm) piece of 24-gauge sterling silver wire
- 8 in. (20cm) pieces of sterling silver chain in different styles (x5)
- 5mm copper freshwater pearls (x2)
- 20mm sterling silver Bali "S" clasp
- 7 in. (17.5cm) piece of sterling silver chain
- 8mm Swarovski crystal ball bead
- 2–3 in. (5–7cm) pieces of mixed chain (x8–10)
- 4mm sterling silver beads (x2)
- Antique steel-cut button

- Mixed beads: crystals stone, pearl, glass, metal (x9–10)
- 1½ in. (4cm) 24-gauge dead-soft sterling silver head pins (x7–10)
- Flexible measuring tape
- Bead board
- Half-round-nose pliers
- Flush cutters
- Chain-nose pliers

Get it right!

To calculate the total length of your finished piece add 3 in. (7.5cm) onto the necklace measurement to allow for how low down the decorative dangles will hang around your neck.

Measuring

Determine the correct measurement you need for your completed piece (see "Measuring Up" on page 19). Lay out your design on the bead board, allowing ¼ in. (5mm) between each element for wire wrapping.

The necklace pictured measures 18 in. (46cm).

Assembling

Cut a 2 in. (5cm) piece of wire and form a loop approximately ¾ in. (2cm) from one end using half-round-nose pliers (see "Wire Wrapping" on page 24).

Slide one end link of each of three 8 in. (20cm) chains into the loop and wire-wrap the loop.

Thread a copper freshwater pearl onto the wire and wire-wrap the opposite end of the wire to one side of the Bali clasp.

Repeat this step for the other side of the clasp, using the remaining two 8 in. (20cm) chains and the 7 in. (14cm) piece of chain (see Fig. 1).

Fig. 1

Cut a 2 in. (5cm) piece of wire and form a loop approximately ¾ in. (2cm) from one end.

Slide on the end link of the 7 in. (18cm) piece of chain and wire-wrap.

Slide the Swarovski ball bead onto this wire and form a loop but do not finish the wire wrapping yet. Set this side of the necklace down.

Wire-wrap a 2 in. (5cm) piece of wire to the other side of the necklace chains.

Slide one sterling-silver bead, the antique steel-cut button, and the second sterling-silver bead onto the wire and form a loop, but do not wire-wrap just yet. Set the necklace aside.

Take your time to arrange bits of chain and beads into links. Wire-wrap beads to each other and to the ends of chain using the 1 ½ in. (4cm) head pins.

Use a piece of scrap wire to see how the chain pieces and bead groupings fall when hanging together.

Make seven to ten dangles.

Finishing

Once you are pleased with your bead and chain arrangements, hook half of them onto the loop beneath the Swarovski ball bead. Wire-wrap the loop to secure.

Hook the remaining chain arrangements onto the loop beneath the antique button.

Before completing the wire wrap, hook the wire-wrap link beneath the Swarovski crystal ball bead into the loop so connecting the two sides to create a sparkling fall of chain and beads in the center of the necklace (see Fig. 2).

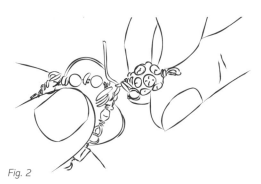

Fig. 2

SPIRAL RELIC EARRINGS

This is a very artistic take on wire wrapping. Not only can you create the ear wires yourself, but the fabric bead has a crafted wire base and a wrapped glass-bead dangle. You can substitute fibers, yarn, handmade paper, and patterned art papers in place of the fabric for different textures and colors. The wire used for this project is in 2 gauges, 20 gauge for the ear wires and the fabric bead base, and 24 gauge for the outside wrap and dangling glass bead. Once you've tried this project in the inexpensive copper wire first, experiment with sterling-silver or gold-filled wire.

Skill level ★ ★ Approximate completion time: **3 hours**

What you need

- 12 in. (30cm) pieces of 20-gauge dead-soft copper wire (x2)
- 4 x 2 in. (10 x 5cm) piece of fabric
- 6 in. (15cm) pieces of 24-gauge dead-soft copper wire (x2)
- 7mm turquoise Czech-glass teardrop beads (x2)
- 8 in. (20cm) pieces of 24-gauge dead-soft copper wire (x2)
- Aqua-colored seed beads in size 11/0 (x30)
- Half-round-nose pliers

- Ruler
- Scissors
- Diamond glaze dimensional adhesive
- Small paintbrush
- Flush cutters
- Chain-nose pliers
- Wire-wrapping jig
- Jeweler's file or emery board

Assembling

Start by making a wire link: Take one piece of 12 in. (30cm) 20-gauge copper wire and form a loop approximately halfway down the wire using half-round-nose pliers (see "Wire Wrapping" on page 24), wrap the copper wire several times until you have a nice thick wrap.

Form another loop approximately 1 in. (2.5cm) away from the first. Wire-wrap this loop until it is as thick as the first. Repeat these two steps to make a second wire link.

Measure the space between the wraps on each wire link—you will use this to calculate how much fabric you need (see Fig. 1).

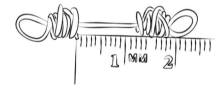

Fig. 1

Cut the fabric you have chosen into two long triangles, where the short edge measures the same width as the space between the wraps on the wire link.

For the project shown, the fabric was ½ in. (1cm) along the base of the triangle with 4 in. (10cm) sides. It does not have to be exact, however, as you can push the fabric in and cut away any extra.

Starting with the widest end, roll the fabric around the wire.

Place a drop of the diamond glaze adhesive under the tip of the fabric and hold in place until the glue sets firm.

Using the small paintbrush, coat the fabric beads with diamond glaze (see Fig. 2) and hang from a piece of scrap wire to dry (about 2 hours).

Fig. 2

Take a 6 in. (15cm) piece of 24-gauge copper wire and wire-wrap a turquoise glass teardrop bead as you did the briolettes in chapter 4 (see page 82).

Form a loop with the doubled wire and thread the loop through the bottom loop of wire link with the fabric bead.

Wire-wrap the loop and trim away the extra wire with the flush cutters.

Repeat with the second turquoise glass teardrop bead.

Finishing

Take an 8 in. (20cm) piece of 24-gauge copper wire and bend it in half at the middle of the wire.

Wind this wire around the base of the fabric bead, directly over the thick wire-wrap you made in step one, using the chain-nose pliers.

As you wind the wire around the fabric bead, slide on the aqua-colored seed beads in a random fashion (see Fig. 3).

Fig. 3

Continue winding the wire around the fabric bead until you reach the top of it, pressing in the end of the wire using the chain-nose pliers.

Create your own ear wires using the wire-wrapping jig and 20-gauge copper wire (see page 117). File smooth the end that goes into your ear using the jeweler's file or emery board.

Alternatively you can use premade ear wires through the top loop of your fabric bead.

Variation

Try linking a handful of these beads together for bracelets and necklaces. Simply join the beads using jump rings; open each, thread two wire-wrapped beads onto the ring, and close again. Keep going until you have the measurement you want. This version also has wire-wrapped pearls between the spiral relics, wire-wrapped and attached in the same way.

OLIVINE DRAPE

This is a truly cosmopolitan piece, perfect for those memorable, glamorous evenings dancing the night away. It's sophisticated, olive-green color is rendered in flashing crystal that captures the light and leads the eye along the graceful lines of the wearer's neck. This sparkling, intricate, woven crystal necklace is put together in layers, first weaving the base of the necklace and then weaving in strands of beads in varying sizes.

Skill level ★ ★ ★   Approximate completion time: **4 hours**

What you need

- Size 11/0 round silver-lined olive seed beads (7gm)
- 12 x 8mm Swarovski Crystal polygon in Olivine (x2)
- 1½ in. (3.8cm) 24-gauge sterling-silver headpin
- 14 in. (35.5cm) 24-gauge dead-soft sterling-silver wire
- 6mm Swarovski crystal bicones in Olivine (x47)
- 4mm Swarovski crystal bicones in Olivine (x141)
- 4mm Swarovski crystal bicones (x88) in Smoked Topaz

- Spool of 0.18 beading wire
- 2 x 2mm sterling-silver crimp beads (x10)
- 15mm two-strand sterling-silver filigree clasp with jump rings attached
- Flexible measuring tape
- Wire cutters
- Flush cutters
- Half-round-nose pliers
- Chain-nose pliers
- Crimping pliers

Preparing

Prepare the center drop ahead of time. Using the half-round-nose pliers, wire-wrap one seed bead, one polygon crystal, and one seed bead onto a head pin (see "Wire Wrapping" on page 24).

Now wire-wrap the following group of beads to this element, using a 2 in. (5cm) piece of the sterling-silver wire for each wrap: One seed bead, one 6mm olivine crystal, and one seed bead.

Repeat this last step twice more with 6mm olivine crystals; once with a 4mm olivine crystal; and three times with smoked topaz crystals. You should end up with a 4¾ in. (12cm) section of wire-wrapped beads for your centerpiece (see Fig. 1).

Fig. 1

Centerpiece

Cut two 25 in. (63.5cm) pieces of beading wire and tie a loose overhand knot approximately 1 in. (2.5cm) from one end of each piece. Thread one strand of beading wire through a 6mm olivine crystal from right to left, and thread the second strand of beading wire through the same crystal from left to right. You should have two ends of beading wire coming out of opposite sides of the crystal bead.

Pull each piece of beading wire until you have approximately 10 in. (25cm) left at each end. At the unknotted end of one strand string the following beads: One seed bead, one 4mm olivine crystal, one seed bead, one 4mm olivine crystal, one seed bead, one 4mm olivine crystal, one seed bead, one 4mm olivine crystal, one seed bead, one 4mm olivine crystal, and one seed bead. Hold this section carefully in your hand while you repeat the same sequence of beads with the second strand of beading wire. You should now have two strands with the same sequence of seed beads and crystals.

Slide the second polygon crystal onto one of the beaded wires, and thread the second beaded wire through the same polygon crystal, heading in the opposite direction. Pull the wires so that all the beads come together into a circle and tie a loose overhand knot at the end of each (see Fig. 2).

Fig. 2

Now return to the two ends of beading wire with overhand knots. Untie the knot on one strand and string exactly the same sequence of beads as you did on the unknotted wires. And repeat again for the second strand of beading wire. Now thread the first strand through a 6mm olivine crystal, and thread the second strand through the same bead, heading in the opposite direction. You will have created a second bead circle. Tie loose overhand knots at the end of the strands coming out of one bead circle (see Fig. 3).

Fig. 3

Working on the beading wires coming out of the second beaded circle, string the following beads: one seed bead, one 4mm olivine crystal, one seed bead, one 6mm olivine crystal, one seed bead, one 4mm olivine crystal, and one seed bead. Repeat this for the second beading wire, finishing with an additional 6mm olivine crystal. Thread the first strand of beading wire through this last 6mm olivine crystal, heading in the opposite direction. Tie loose overhand knots in the ends of the beading wires.

Untie the loose overhand knots at the ends of the beading wires from the first beaded circle. Repeat

the previous step with this side of the necklace to form another circle and tie loose overhand knots at the end of the beading wires. You will now have four woven crystal circles at the center of your necklace—the centerpiece (see Fig. 4).

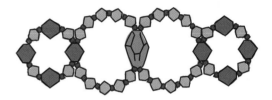

Fig.4

Crystal circles

Having established the centerpiece for your necklace, you will now continue to string the left-hand side of the necklace in the same way until your measurement reaches 6½ in. (16.5cm) from the central polygon crystal. Remember to knot the ends of the wires as you complete each circle.

Repeat the following sequence five times to create five more circles on the left-hand side of the necklace. String one strand of beading wire with one seed bead, one 4mm olivine crystal, one seed bead, one 4mm olivine crystal, one seed bead, one 4mm olivine crystal, one seed bead, one 4mm olivine crystal, and one seed bead. String the same sequence on the second strand, plus an additional 6mm olivine crystal. Thread the first strand through the 6mm olivine crystal heading in

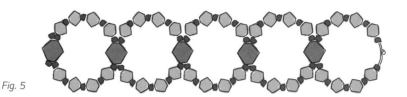

Fig. 5

the opposite direction. On nearing completion on the fifth circle, do not end with the 6mm olivine crystal, but simply tie overhand knots in the strands of beading wire (see Fig. 5). (Later on these will be crimped onto the two-strand clasp.)

Repeat all of the crystal circle steps for the right-hand side of the necklace. You should now have approximately 13 in. (34cm) of woven crystal circles—six circles on either side of the centerpiece (see Fig. 6).

Fig. 6

Center drop

Cut a 24 in. (61cm) piece of beading wire. Working in the center of the necklace, and from left to right, thread the wire through the first 4mm bead below the large polygon crystal on the left-hand side, string on a seed bead, and thread the wire through the first 4mm bead below the large polygon crystal on the right-hand side. Pull the wire through until the center of the wire is centered beneath the polygon crystal (see Fig. 7).

On the right-hand piece of beading wire string the following sequence of beads: One seed bead, one 6mm olivine crystal, one seed bead, one 6mm

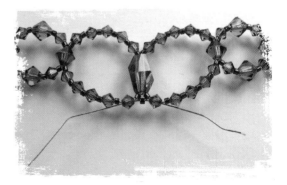

Fig. 7

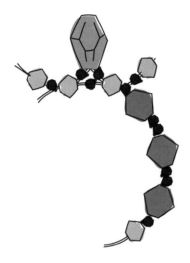

Fig. 8

Fig. 9

crystal, two seed beads, one 6mm crystal, two seed beads, one 6mm crystal, one seed bead, and one 4mm olivine crystal (see Fig. 8). Slide on the top wire-wrapped loop of the center drop you made in preparation and tie a loose overhand knot at the end of the beading wire. Repeat the beading sequence for the left-hand piece of beading wire, threading the end of the wire through the top loop of the wire-wrapped center drop (see Fig. 9).

Assembling

Working on the right-hand wire, string one 4mm topaz crystal and one seed bead alternately until you have strung nine of each. String one 6mm olivine crystal and continue alternating seed beads and topaz crystals until you have strung nine more

crystals and ten seed beads. After the tenth seed bead, string one 6mm olivine crystal and four more 4mm topaz crystal with seed beads in between (see Fig. 10). Finish with crimp bead (see "Crimping" on page 20).

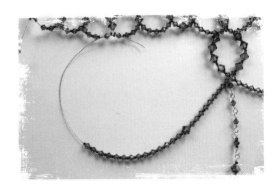

Fig. 10

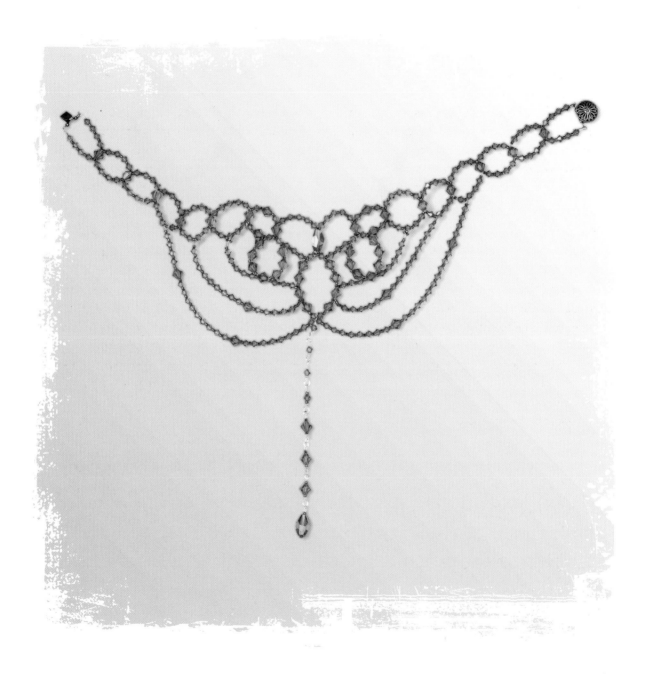

Still working on the right-hand wire, you now need to thread this through the two 4mm olivine crystals just below the 6mm olivine crystal between the third and fourth woven crystal circles you made in previous steps (counting from the unfinished end). Work from right to left, and thread on a seed bead as you come out of the right-hand crystal and before going into the left-hand crystal. Repeat the previous steps on the left-hand wire.

Cut a 20 in. (51cm) piece of beading wire. Working on the right-hand side of the necklace, and from right to left, thread this wire through the two 4mm olivine crystals just below the 6mm olivine crystal between the first and second woven crystal circles you made (counting from the centerpiece). You need to string on a seed bead as you come out of the first crystal and before going into the second. Pull the wire through until you have 5 in. (12.5cm) on the left-hand side of the bead and 15 in. (38cm) on the right-hand side (see Fig. 11).

On the 5 in. (12.5cm) end of the wire, string one seed bead, one 6mm olivine crystal, one seed bead, one 6mm olivine crystal, one seed bead, one 6mm olivine crystal, and one seed bead. Tie a loose overhand knot and set this wire piece down. String the same sequence of beads onto the 15 in. (38cm) end of the wire, adding an additional 6mm olivine crystal. Tie a loose overhand knot and set this piece down.

Now push the end of the 5 in. (12.5cm) wire through the additional 6mm olivine crystal, from right to left. Pull it tight, and string five topaz crystals with seed beads in between, followed by a crimp bead and one seed bead. Thread the wire through the bottom crystal of the third circle that you made in step 8 (counting from the centerpiece). Slide on a seed bead before pushing the wire back into the crimp bead, pulling tight

Fig. 11

Fig. 12

with the chain-nose pliers, and crimping the wire to the necklace (see Fig. 12).

Repeat all of the assembly steps on the left-hand side of the necklace.

Return to the 15 in. (38cm) end of the wire on the right-hand side of the necklace. String on one seed bead, one 4mm topaz crystal, one seed bead, one topaz crystal, one seed bead, one topaz crystal, and one seed bead. Push the bead wire through the third 6mm olivine bead down from the bottom of the centerpiece on the right-hand side (see Fig. 13).

Fig. 13

String on four seed beads, then string one seed bead between each of the crystals in the following order: One 4mm olivine crystal, four topaz crystals, one 6mm olivine crystal, four topaz crystals, one 4mm olivine crystal, and four topaz crystals, before

sliding on a crimp bead. Tie a knot at the end and repeat these steps with the 15 in. (38cm) piece of wire on the opposite side of the necklace (see Fig.14).

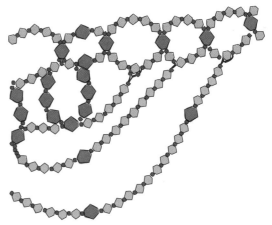

Fig. 14

Working on the right-side of the necklace, count from the centerpiece to the second and third crystal circle that you made. Count down three 4mm olivine crystals from the 6mm olivine crystal, in between the second and third crystal circle. Working from left to right, thread your beading wire through this third crystal. Pull the wire through completely and thread back into the crimp bead, tighten with the chain-nose pliers, then crimp the crimp bead with the crimping pliers. Repeat this step with the left-hand side of the necklace (see Fig. 15).

Fig. 15

Get it right!

Before finishing your woven crystal necklace, check the woven circles, tightening each of them by pulling gently on the wires. This will close the circles completely, preventing any gaps or warps in the weaving.

Finishing

In order to make sure that you crimp each strand of your beaded wire to the correct jump ring on the two-strand clasp, lay the necklace flat on your work surface. Start with the top strand on the right-hand side. Untie the overhand knot and slide on a crimp bead. Loop the beading wire through the jump ring at the top-right side of the clasp and back down into the crimp bead. Pull tight with the chain-nose pliers and crimp with the crimping pliers. Repeat this process with the bottom strand on the right-hand side.

Keeping the necklace flat on your work surface, untie the overhand knot on the top strand of the left-hand side, slide on a crimp bead, and loop the wire through the jump ring at the top-left side the clasp. Thread the wire back down into the crimp bead, pull tight with the chain-nose pliers and crimp. Repeat this process with the bottom strand on the left-hand side (see Fig. 16).

Fig. 16

RESOURCES AND SUPPLIERS

While most basic beading materials can be found at your local craft store, you will invariably find yourself searching for more unique beads and findings. I have compiled a list of dependable businesses that work hard to ensure you receive quality goods at reasonable prices with quick shipping and excellent customer service.

Seed beads, glass beads, crystals, semi-precious stones, findings, and tools;
Fire Mountain Gems and Beads
One Fire Mountain Way
Grants Pass, Oregon
97526-2373, USA
www.firemountaingems.com

Vintage Lucite beads, lockets, chains, and findings;
The Beadin' Path
15 Main Street
Freeport, Maine
04032, USA
www.beadinpath.com

Filigree brass medallions, hammered circle links, and bead caps;
The Mermaids Dowry
www.mermaidsdowry.etsy.com

The Despina Collection
www.thedespinacollection.etsy.com

Enameled flower findings;
Wendy Baker Design
www.sleepingdogstudio.etsy.com

Hill Tribe Silver;
Karen Silver of Thailand
2 Thaikarensilver-house
145/1 Karen Hill Tribe Village
T.Omkoi A.Omkoi
Chiangmai, 50310, Thailand
www.thaikarensilver-house.org

Custom crocheted pod flowers;
Lily Knitting
www.lilyknitting.etsy.com

INDEX

DISCARD

Credits

Art Direction: Simon Daley and Richard Dewing

Designer: Sharanjit Dhol

Illustrator: Stefanie Coltra

Photographer: Sussie Ahlburg

Additional photography supplied by the author

Models: Genevieve Carden, Nicola Coates, Stefanie Coltra, Victoria Dewing, Ester Keate, Margarita Lievano Mosquera, Mafalda Satz, Sarah Taylor, Nhuc Tran, Marisa Wasboonma